Fakie

About the author

TONY VARRATO

Tony grew up in Millsboro, Delaware in the USA and graduated from the University of Delaware in 1988. He has taught in Vineland NJ, Selbyville DE and Georgetown, DE. He is both an author and high school English teacher who knows his audience well. He wrote this novel specifically for the reluctant readers in his classroom, and others like them. In his words, "They wanted something fast-paced, action-packed, and short." In addition to his first novel, 'Fakie', he is also the author of 'Outrage' and likes to connect with his readers through his MySpace page and website, tonyvarrato.com. When not teaching or writing he enjoys getting outside as much as possible, kayaking, running, hiking, skiing, biking and trying to learn skateboarding from his own kids!

Tony Varrato

Fakie

Teen Readers

Tony Varrato
Fakie
Teen Readers, level 3

Illustrations: Niels Roland
Edited by: Pye Tosti

Series editors: Stine Benzon and Ulla Malmmose

Cover layout: Mette Plesner
Cover photo: SeventyFour/iStock/Getty Images Plus

ISBN Denmark: 978-87-23-54134-5
www.easyreaders.eu

Easy Readers
EGMONT

Printed in Denmark

Alex Miller: His real name is Danny Torbert. Alex is the current false identity being used by Danny. He is a teenage boy and witness in a murder case. Both Danny and his mom are in a witness protection programme. Alex is a skater.

Eileen: Mrs Torbert and Danny's mother. She is also a witness in the murder case. She now calls herself Sonya Miller.

Tim: One of Alex's new skateboarder friends and a student at his new school.

Brian: First Brian is the school bully, but later he becomes Alex's new friend. He's a big fan of four wheel motor biking.

Steve: A former friend of Danny's father and in prison for his murder. He used to be an agent of the FBI.

Frank: Steve's man on the outside of prison, trying to find Alex and Sonya for Steve.

Aaron: A friend of Frank's. He is a professional 'hit man' and will try to kill Alex and Sonya.

Gina: Another friend of Frank's, also trying to find Alex and Sonya to kill them. She is a professional killer.

Lankford: An FBI agent, head of the witness protection programme. He creates the false identities and arranges places for FBI witnesses to hide.

Chapter 1

They always left in a different direction. This time, they were going south. It was early morning when they left. He looked at his watch. It was 3:07 a.m. as the car rolled down the highway.

His mom broke the silence. "So, have you decided who you're going to be this time?"

He thought for a minute - it was best to think before answering. If he had done that in the first place, he and his mom wouldn't be in this mess.

"I think I'd like to be a skateboarder."

"I guess you'll have to learn a few new words then. You'll be saying *'dude'* and 'like' all the time", she smiled.

"Yeah, you're right, mom I know a few words already though. But I'll need some new clothes like *baggy pants,* loose t-shirts and of course, a skateboard. That's what the *skaters* wear on the videos I've been watching on YouTube."

"How are you going to cut your hair? You need it long in front, don't you?"

"Yeah, I think I'll let my hair grow longer. Maybe I'll get it *straightened.* Any idea of your job this time, mom?"

"I want us to live near the beach. Maybe a pizza bar this time."

His mom would only take jobs in restaurants, where she was paid cash. She needed as much cash as possible. They

---

dude [djuːd], American slang for a young man
baggy pants, loose trousers like jogging pants
skater ['skeɪtə], name given to a person who likes skateboarding
straightened ['streɪtənd], the opposite of curly

always had to be ready to leave an area very quickly – just like tonight. There would be no time to go to a bank or a cash machine for money. Also a cash machine left videos of each *transaction*. It would be too dangerous for them.

Last time they moved he had shaved his head to fit in with the rest of the football team. That all went very well until last night. The problem was that he had made a great goal in last night's game. His *teammates* and the audience thought it was fantastic, all he could think was: What have I done? The local newspaper had showed his picture on the front page this morning, so they had no choice but to leave as soon as it got dark.

Another life ended, and a new life was ready to begin. How many lives had this been? Was it seven or eight? His real name didn't matter anymore. He could never be the person he was before all this had happened — and he didn't want to. His mom was just **Mom**, he was her son, and Dad was dead. That's all there was to it.

"Do we have a last name yet?" he asked his mom.

"What about Miller? It's common, but it's not too common."

"Great. I was afraid we were going to call ourselves Smith, Jones, and Johnson or something like that," he said with a smile.

"Hey, I'm getting better at this. I just hope we don't have to move too much in the *future*."

---

transaction [træn'zækʃn], taking money out of a cash machine
teammates, the other people on your team e.g. soccer
future ['fju:tʃə], opposite of past

"Well, if we get into trouble, we'll just have to call Mr. Lankford."

Mom was silent.

"As a last way out of course," he added.

"Yes, it has to be a very last way out," she said.

Chapter 2

The state prison outside Chicago was *tough.* There were very few fights and no escapes as there were too many guards watching the *prisoners.* Frank hated coming here. He could feel the fear and his heart pumping hard. He was afraid to get locked up himself one day. Well, so far he was only visiting. Frank realized that the guards didn't *scare* him as much as the man he was visiting. What scared him the most was the ways Steve Ballantine could reach Frank, even though he was locked up in prison.

"Hello, good to see you, how's everybody?" Steve said in an ice cold voice.

"Steve, we think we saw him in a local New York newspaper three days ago. We've sent the girls out to check it out. He was playing football, and there was a big photo of him on the front page."

"You don't think they're stupid enough to stay there, do you?" Steve clearly thought Frank was an idiot. Then again, Steve thought everybody were idiots.

"No, Steve, no. We think they've left already. But we'll do the usual search. We're sure they'll make a mistake at some point."

Steve leaned forward and looked Frank straight in the eye. "I want them found. Do you understand!? Two years in this place is too much."

He leaned back in his chair. "So, how's my business doing?"

---

tough [tʌf], hard
prisoner ['prɪzənə], person in jail for a crime
to scare, to frighten or to be afraid

Three days were enough to set up a new life. Alex and Sonya Miller were now real people living in a small house only nineteen minutes from Virginia Beach. Alex's mom was busy working on the computer Mr. Lankford had given to them. Soon she had printed out a *driver's license, social security cards* and *birth certificates.* Alex was still nervous about his first day at a new school even though he had started school twice before this year. He looked at his new clothes to make sure everything was ok before he left for school. He went out to their "new" car. They had sold their old car and bought this old white Toyota for eight hundred dollars cash. They liked to buy old cars because no one wanted to steal them. And besides – buying an old car with cash doesn't leave a *trail* behind you for anyone to follow.

When they arrived at the school the school day had already begun. Most people were already in their classes. Mrs. Wisniewski, the school secretary, was glad that Alex Miller had all his personal papers with him. She wrote his information straight into her database, printed out his *timetable,* and sent Alex off to his class.

Alex was always surprised that even before he had stepped into a classroom, everyone knew he was coming.

---

driver's license ['laɪsəns] document showing you are allowed to drive a car
social security [sɪ'kjʊərəti] *card,* national insurance number allowing you to work in the USA
birth certificate [sə'tɪfɪkət], document showing when and where you were born
trail [treɪl], signs left by a person e.g. a footprint
timetable, list of class times and classroom numbers

Text messaging would easily spread the news. The next two days were going to be difficult, they usually were.

Luckily, he saw a few others with a skater look. On his way to his seat, he gave two of them a friendly smile.

Alex talked to some of the other skaters between the lessons. He studied how they walked, the words they used, and their body language. These students seemed to be much friendlier than the kids in some of the other schools he had gone to. He must have got his new look right after all.

Some of the students who were checking him out were girls. He looked back at a few of them, but he didn't do too much. It was too soon. He wished this was three days from now, when he wasn't "the new boy" any more.

The first *troublemaker* came along on the way back from lunch. A large *guy* bumped into Alex. He looked him straight in the eye as he slowly passed him in the hallway.

Alex knew this type of idiot very well – he had been one of them just last week.

In those few seconds, a small crowd had come together to see if it was time to watch a good fight. Alex just smiled and walked towards his classroom. He knew better than that. It gives too much *publicity* to start a fight. Too many people want to test tough guys. He used to be one tough guy himself when they first moved.

This guy was going to be a problem. Alex would have to *deal with* him soon.

---

troublemaker, somebody who is always starting fights
guy [gaɪ], American expression for a man or a boy
publicity [pʌbˈlɪsɪti], advertising
to deal with, to do business with or solve a problem

Chapter 4

Alex picked up his new skateboard. He put his right foot on the board and pushed off with his left. There wasn't much room in their new garage, so he had to *practice carving.* That seemed easy enough, but he had to keep doing it until he felt comfortable. Once he had the carving under control, it was time to practice his *ollie.* He *slammed* his back foot on the back of the deck and jumped. Nothing happened. This would take a lot of work.

His mother came home at about 11 that night. By that time, Alex was ready for bed. It had been a long day after all.

She came into his room "Well, how was school today?"

"It was a typical first day. I dressed right, the teachers seem ok, and I met the first *bully,* I think."

"What are you going to do about him?" she asked.

"The usual," he said with a *confident* smile. He didn't want his mom to get too worried.

---

to practice, the effort to get better at something
carving ['kɑːvɪŋ], turning from side to side
Ollie, see skateboarder slang, p. 26-27
to slam, here it is to push down hard with your foot
bully ['bʊli], coward, somebody who fights younger or smaller people
to be confident ['kɒnfɪdnt], to believe in yourself

Chapter 5

A few days later Frank was back visiting Steve in the prison.

"You were right, Steve, no result! We've found out the type of car and the *license plate number*, but she's sold that car already." Frank leaned in a little closer to Steve, like he wanted to ask: "So, what's your next idea, boss?"

"I need a map," Steve said. "Mark every place we know they've stayed and write down every move they've made on that map. There has to be a *pattern* to their movements." Steve *grit-ted* his teeth. "It would be nice for you guys to find out where they are now, instead of always being one step behind."

Day two is always the worst, Alex thought. You're still the new kid, but now everyone wants to get all the information they can about you. Of course, Alex couldn´t tell anything about his past. "You can't hide from yourself!" He remembered that old song very well. His dad used to play it all the time.

It brought up memories, to think about that song. Memories that *flashed* at him, memories he didn't want to come back: the *explosion* of the gun and the silent scream.

"I'm sorry, Dad." Oh, no, he couldn't cry now. He had to pull himself together.

A boy his own age stopped in front of Alex in the hallway.

---

license plate number, number plate on front and back of car
pattern [ˈpætən], series of clues that help solve a puzzle or mystery
to grit, to put your teeth together
to flash, to show for a second
explosion [ɪkˈspləʊʒn], noise from a gun or bomb

"If you read that *magazine* in class, the teachers will take it from you," he said.

The skate magazine in Alex's hand had worked. He had got the attention he wanted from the right kind of guy.

"Yeah, that's because, they're all skaters themselves" Alex smiled.

"Yeah, especially Mr. Jackson. I *bet* at night, when no one's around, he is on a skateboard himself."

They both laughed, and with that, Alex made his first friend in this life.

"My name's Tim."

"I'm Alex."

"Yeah, I know. You're in three of my classes."

"Cool."

"Hey!" a loud voice said from behind them. Mr. Tough Guy from the day before made his way towards Tim and Alex." You two look cute together don't you, ha, ha." The guy laughed and walked into Tim's class.

Alex and Tim watched him for a moment.

They both just shook their heads. "Who is this guy and who is the small guy who always seems to follow?" Alex asked.

"The loud one is Brian, and his friend is Carl. They give everybody a hard time. You just get extra attention because you're new," Tim said.

Alex nodded.

---

magazine [ˌmægəˈziːn], small book e.g. about sport or fashion
to bet, to be certain

"I'd like to kick him at his *backside* and stick him in a *locker*, but he probably wouldn't fit." Tim shook his head and picked up his books.

Alex liked Tim already. Most kids would have been scared for the rest of the day after this. Tim was smart enough to forget about stupid comments and get on with his life.

backside ['bæksaɪd], bottom
locker, cupboard to keep clothes in, usually in a gym

Chapter 6

"Alex."

Alex jumped up from the sofa. "Oh, I must have fallen asleep," he said with a smile.

"You don't have to wait up for me every night, you know," his mother said.

"Yeah, I know," he answered. "I just feel better knowing you're home."

"I know what you mean; I feel the same way while you're at school. I'm always afraid this will be the day someone finds out," Sonya said.

She sat down on the sofa next to him. "So, how was school? How is practice going?"

"Practice is going well. I finally got the Ollie right. School is ok. The classes are very much the same as at the other schools but that bully is still giving me a bit of trouble. I really don't want a fight right now," Alex said.

"You know that you need to be careful," his mom said. "Remember, we had to leave our second identity because you were playing around with bullies. That got very messy, very quickly."

"Yeah," Alex said. "I thought about that." He remembered that life very well. Full of fights that was.

"Don't worry mom, I want to *handle* this quickly and quietly," he promised.

"Just be careful, son." She put her hand on his shoulder. "Now, it's time for bed."

---

to handle, to take care of a situation

"Hey, Alex, what are you doing after school?" Tim asked on the way to their classroom the next morning.

"Not much. Why?"

"Me, Nate, and Tyler are going to build a *skate ramp* in my garden."

"Cool! You mean a big one?"

"Yeah, we're using some old wood. My dad's got a lot of tools. We just need to find out how to build the thing."

The word "dad" still hit Alex like a *punch*, even after all these years. He hoped his face didn't show.

"That sounds good to me. What time?"

"We're going right after school. Do you need to ask your parents?"

"Yeah," Alex said. "I'll have to help my mom first since we're still moving in and all that. Will you guys still be working around 5:30?"

"Yeah, my mom's getting pizza, so we can work through dinner," Tim said.

"I'll be there," Alex said. He couldn't help smiling.

Basketball ended at 5 pm that day. Brian had started his walk home, after he had been bullying some of the younger kids as usual. He cut across the parking area and into the woods. He lived on a farm only a mile away from school.

Something moved in the corner of Brian's eye, but he didn't have a chance to see what it was before he was on the ground. Then, suddenly he couldn't breathe.

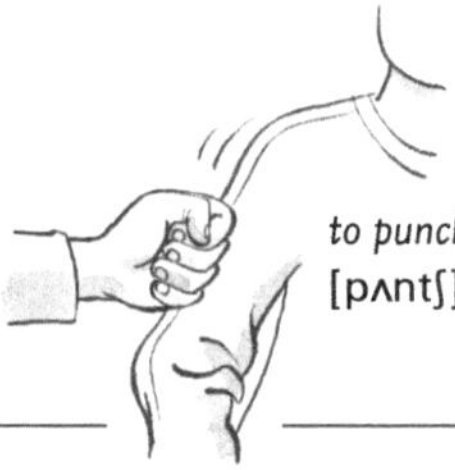

to punch
[pʌntʃ]

---

skate ramp, platform for skaters to jump in the air

2 *

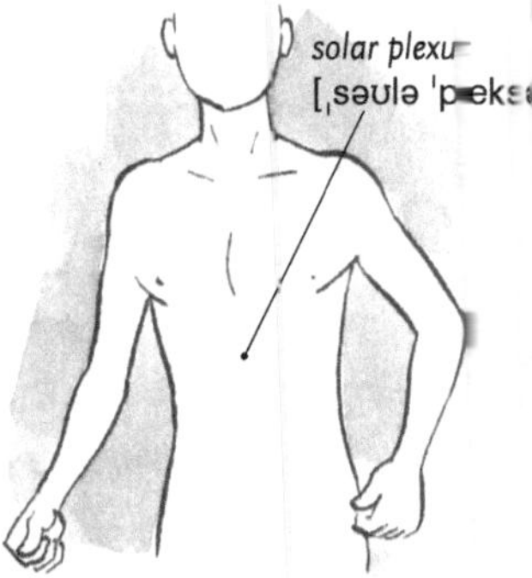

"That's your *solar plexus*, Brian."

"Auhh," Brian screamed.

"Now, I don't want any more trouble with you, ok! If I do, I'll have to show this in *public*, right!!" He left Brian, who was finally starting to breathe normally.

Alex was smiling as he got onto his bike. That was almost too easy, he thought. He believed that he had given Brian something to think about.

"Denver, Colorado; Tennessee; Minneapolis, Minnesota; Texas; Utah; Phoenix, Arizona; New York," Frank was pointing at a map. The locations were only marked with small *dots*, so the guards wouldn't notice. "There's no real pattern," he said to Steve.

"Use Google Earth to zoom down and look for their car!" Steve said. Frank took a deep breath. "It doesn't work like that," he explained. "Google Earth's satellite pictures don't show live action. They can be months, sometimes years old.

"Don't we have someone who can get us live pictures?" Steve was angry.

"We're working on it. But even if we look into old *footage* from many different satellites it could take longer than we have," Frank shook his head.

"Then you'd better find their pattern before my *appeal date*."

---

public [ˈpʌblɪk], in front of people
dot, round pencil marks for instance.
footage [ˈfʊtɪdʒ], video pictures
appeal [əˈpiːl] *date*, appearance in court to try and get out of jail

"So, what do we do? Just guess their next stop?" Frank was getting *desperate.*

"No," Steve shouted. "We look at the areas where they haven't been yet. That would be this area here," Steve was pointing at the East Coast on the map.

"That doesn't make it much easier," Frank protested.

"It does, since they have already been up north. They will go somewhere in the middle here, like Maryland, Virginia, or Carolina."

"That's a lot to cover," Frank said. He was getting really angry.

"That's why you need some help from the girls, and maybe even some help from the *FBI.*"

---

to be desperate ['despərət], to feel hopeless
FBI, Federal Bureau of Investigation, USA law agency

Tom Lankford had been with the FBI for twenty-seven years. The first eleven years he had been working around drugs and *drug dealers.* He had really liked that job. It had been full of *excitement,* especially when bullets went *whizzing* past his head during a *raid.* But he didn't want to take the risk any more. He didn't want to leave his wife and leave his kids without a dad.

Now Lankford worked in a *Witness Protection Program.* He liked that job, too. He loved making up names and histories; with his computer, he could easily make new birth certificates, death certificates, marriage certificates and social security numbers. He felt like a *magician,* making people appear and disappear.

He told no one about his clients. It was the safest way to keep them alive. For the last sixteen years, he had never lost one client. He was their lifeline. Lankford advised his clients only to contact him in case of *emergency.* Also, they only had contact through e-mail. Phone calls were too easy to *trace.*

Lankford packed his bag and walked to the front door of the building. No one had needed his lifeline today.

---

drug dealer, person who sells drugs
excitement [ɪkˈsaɪtmənt], stimulation or feeling really good
to whiz [wɪz], to go very fast
raid [reɪd], police visit to your home
witness protection program, giving new identities to people in danger from criminals
magician [məˈdʒɪʃən], someone who can do magic
emergency [ɪˈmɜːdʒənsi], urgent situation like a car crash
to trace, to try to find

"Goodnight," he said to the security guard in the hall.

"Goodnight, Lankford."

He stopped in front of his car and looked around for any sign of danger, but no danger that day either. Oh dear, how he missed the drug raids and the excitement.

Many cars away, Lankford's killer watched him through his *binoculars.*

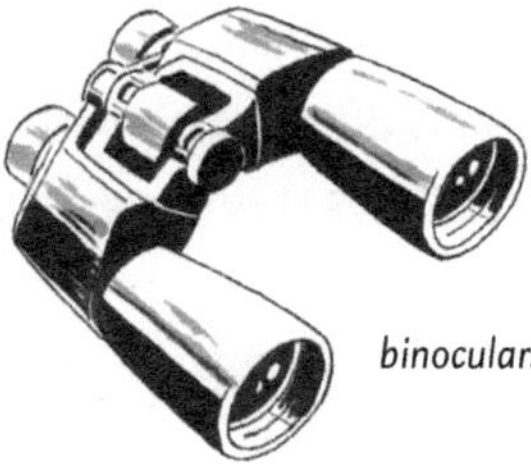

binoculars [bɪ'nɒkjʊləz]

Chapter 8

"Have you guys finished yet, or what?" Alex parked his bike and walked towards his friends.

"Hardly," Tim said. "This ramp is turning into an *amusement park*."

"Well, if we're going to do this," added Tyler, "I think we should go all the way and build a killer *half pipe*."

"But isn't there a skate park ten miles down the road?" Alex asked with a smile.

"Yeah, you're right," Nate said, "and it's pretty cool. But a lot of people use it, so it often gets very busy."

"Anyway," Tim said, "this is turning into a really big project."

Tim looked at the space where the skate ramp would be. "It won't be cheap," he finally said.

"Maybe we can get some of the stuff from a *junkyard*. Do you have one around here?" Alex asked.

"We should take Alex to *Mount Trashmore* on Saturday, so he can see what we're going for," Nate said.

"Great idea! Alex, are you up for it?" asked Tim.

Alex tried to *hide* his *pride*. He was in. He really wanted to

---

amusement [ə'mju:zmənt] *park*, park where young people can have fun
half pipe, see skateboarder slang, p. 26-27
junkyard ['dʒʌŋkjɑ:d], place where old cars are broken up
Mount Trashmore, skateboarder name for the bowl they practice in
to hide, to put somewhere secret
pride, a feeling that you have done good

be one of them. But he knew it couldn't last. It never did.

"Saturday's great, he smiled."

"Can I help you?" The secretary at a Maryland high school asked with a friendly voice.

"Yes, my name is Rachel Phillips and I'm from the *Department of Education*," Gina lied. She was dressed in a nice *blue suit* that would be easy to forget about. "I need some information about any of your students who have started at this school within the last month."

"Why? Is there a problem?"

"No," Gina said with a very friendly smile. "We are just making a *survey*."

"Well, I'll find someone you can speak to," the secretary said. "Good luck with your work."

"Thanks," Gina said. Good luck was needed. This was the first of the five schools she had to visit today. It could take months to find that *little punk!*

Department of Education, state organization dealing with schools and universities
blue suit [sjuːt], jacket and trousers combination
survey [ˈsɜːveɪ], investigation
little punk [pʌŋk], slang term for a kid

Chapter 9

Alex had been practicing a lot over the last three nights. He had searched the Internet for skateboarding tricks and had found the site called "Basic Tricks Every Beginner Should Know." He still wasn't perfect, but at least he had tried a few tricks by now. After all, he had only been a skateboarder for a week.

His mom was happy to let him go to Virginia Beach on Saturday morning. They would cycle to the beach, *hang out* there for a while, and then go to the skate park for the rest of the day. His mom told him to be careful and gave him a kiss – in front of his friends. Then she put forty dollars in his pocket, which almost made it up for that kiss!!

When they got to Atlantic Avenue, Alex was *in the lead.* He could see the ocean for the first time in this life. He was excited. They parked their bikes near a pizza shop. The shop was closed for a few more hours, so they decided to get on their skateboards.

to hang out, to be together
to be in the lead [li:d], to be in front of other people in a race

On Saturdays, the *sidewalks* were reserved for skateboarders and *roller bladers.*

"Come on," said Nate. "Let's go to the *boardwalk* first."

All Alex noticed were girls walking around in less clothes than they wore in the other towns he had lived in.

"Dude," said Tyler. "Haven't you been to the beach before?"

"Uh, no," replied Alex, he *blushed* for the second time this morning. "I haven't."

"Ok, but try not to stare. You're a *local* now."

Alex nodded. "Let's skate."

They began skating down the bike path. They *jumped some curbs* and *ollied* over a few cement blocks. Nate showed Alex a few techniques. "You have to learn to get your balance before you can grind," he explained.

For lunch they had a pizza each and then went into a skate shop.

"I like these long boards," Alex said.

"They're like *surfboards,* though," Tim told him.

"Do you guys surf, too?" Alex asked. He felt like a tourist.

"No," Tim answered. "But there's a great surf camp up in Delaware. You stay there all week and have campfires and stuff. My mom said I can go this summer if I get a job to pay for it."

"That sounds cool."

---

sidewalk, footpath
roller blader, person who likes roller skating
boardwalk ['bɔːdwɔːk], wooden walkway usually by the sea
to blush [blʌʃ], to become red in the face, to be embarrassed
local ['ləʊkəl], from this town
to jump curbs and do Ollies, see skateboarder slang, p. 26-27
surfboard ['sɜːfbɔːd], boards for surfing waves

"Do you want to go?" Tim asked.

Alex nodded. He realized he had made his first *long-term* promise in three years. He hoped he could keep it.

Later on they went out to the skate park. Alex was shocked when he saw the size of it.

"It's really big, isn't it?"

"It's a *landfill*. That's why it's called Mount Trashmore. They dumped a ton of garbage, and then they covered it up, and made it a park," Tyler explained.

"Cool," said Alex.

"Let's try the *bowl* first," suggested Nate.

"Dude!" Tyler said and took out his mobile phone. "Let's film each other for YouTube," he suggested.

"Cool!"

Alex spent his time on the street course, and well away from cameras. He was watching other skaters and tried to copy some of their tricks. YES!! He had landed his first *frontside 180!!* It felt as if he had just *conquered* the world.

---

long-term, over many years in the future
landfill, rubbish tip
bowl [bəʊl], a large hole built in the ground for skating
frontside 180, see skateboarder slang, p. 26-27
to conquer [ˈkɒŋkə], to win or to overcome

"Hey, how are you doing?" Tim asked when they met outside school on Monday morning after a great weekend.

"Are you *sore* from Saturday?"

"Yeah, a little," Alex said. "Mostly my legs."

Tim nodded. "Yeah and my sides are sore, too. I think I might have overdone the bowl."

This identity felt so much better than the others, Alex thought. His new friends felt like real friends. It even felt as if he could open up and be himself. Well, as open as a person could be when he still had to lie about nearly every detail of his life.

"Pay attention," Brian shouted as he pushed little John into an open locker. Brian looked up and got a bit nervous when he saw Alex.

That was only for a few seconds though. Then Brian returned to be Mr. Tough Guy and made his way into the classroom.

"What was that?" asked Tim.

"What?"

"Just that I think Brian stopped *picking on* you pretty quickly after you first got here. What's up?"

"I guess he just knows I'd kick his butt," Alex said with a confident smile.

---

to be sore [sɔː], muscles hurting from doing e.g. sports
to pick on, to bully

"Yeah," Tim added. "I'm sure that's it." They both laughed.

"All right, everyone. Let's take our seats," Mr. Henry was ready to start his lesson.

That's when Alex saw Mike take something from behind his back and place it in the *bin*.

It took three minutes before the *firecrackers* went off. Most of the students were hiding under their desks. Everyone apart from Brian, that was.

Mr. Henry looked up from behind his desk and saw that the only student who didn't move was Brian Joseph! Of course, he had to be the *guilty* one. "Go down to the office right now Brian," he shouted!

"Me? What did I do?"

"Oh, come on, Brian! You're the only one who didn't move! If you didn't set off the firecracker, I'm sure you know who did!

"This is not fair!" *protested* Brian.

The class was silent. Brian stood alone, waiting for someone to help him. The rest of the students were back in their seats. They didn't laugh, as they normally would when Brian had been up to something. Instead, they all stared at Brian.

They all think he's guilty! Alex realized. No, not all, Mike had a smile on his face.

They all started *whispering* when Brian left.

"That was strange! Do you think he's coming back?" Tim whispered.

"Yeah," Alex whispered back. "Because he didn't do it."

---

bin, waste paper basket
firecracker ['faɪəˌkrækə], small but noisy firework
to be guilty ['gɪltɪ], to be convicted of a crime
to protest [prə'test], to object
to whisper ['wɪspə], to speak softly

"You must be joking! What are you talking about?" Tim whispered.

"Shhhh! I watched Mike put it in the bin."

"Why didn't you say something?"

"I ... uh ... I'm the new kid, and I don't need anybody thinking I'm ...."

"I didn't think you *cared* much about what other people thought," Tim said.

---

to care, here: to worry about

"I just don't want people to think I'm friendly with that idiot?"

"Yeah, that one I'll buy," smiled Tim.

The killer looked through his binoculars as Lankford kissed his wife and got into his car. Aaron wrote: "Tuesday, November 23, 7:38 a.m.: Lankford leaves for work."

He let Lankford drive off before he was following. He knew where his *target* was going. Lankford would stop at a local coffee shop to get a coffee, a cake, and a paper. Then he would drive off to work. Every few seconds, Lankford would look around for guys who were waiting to *attack* him. Unfortunately for Lankford, those *fears* were going to become a *reality*.

---

target [ˈtɑːgɪt], something to aim at
to attack [əˈtæk], to start a fight
fears, worries
reality [rɪˈælɪti], real event

Chapter 11

Gym was great; Alex loved playing all sorts of sports on the beach. The problem was the showers after the gym lessons. He always kept his back to the shower wall to cover his chest scars with soap as quickly as possible. He was showered and dressed within minutes.

He looked at himself in the mirror. He was letting his hair grow a little longer now, mostly in the front, like Tyler's. Above all, he had to fit in with the skater guys.

Suddenly he could hear the door being locked behind him.

"Miller!" Alex got really nervous!

It was Brian!

"Alex, I know you were the one who helped me out of the firecracker situation. I've been thinking a lot about it, and it had to be you. I just wanted to say thanks," Brian said.

"Don't worry about it," Alex answered without a smile. He couldn't have Brian thinking he was soft. "You didn't do it, so there was no reason for you to get the *blame*. But don't think this makes us friends or anything."

"Of course not," Brian said, as they both walked out. "I don't want any skate friends."

"Fine by me. So hey, when you're not beating people up, what do you do for fun?"

"I ride my *four-wheeler* through the woods," Brian smiled.

"Oh, yeah? I used to do that," Alex smiled back. "A friend of mine had one that could race at eighty miles an hour. He broke

---

blame, responsibility
four-wheeler, motorbike with four wheels

both of his arms though. He looked like a cactus with his *casts* on."

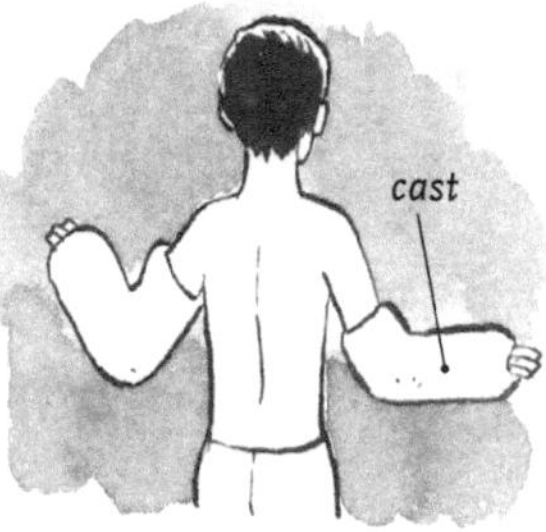

Brian laughed. "I've got one that races too. I've never broken my arms, but I've come pretty close —I've *flipped* it a couple of times. You can come over and try to break your arms sometime if you want."

Alex smiled. "Yeah, that would be cool."

As they got into the hallway with the rest of the students, Brian was back to being tough. "Of course we're still not friends."

"Of course not," Alex agreed!

On Monday afternoon Alex, Tim, Nate, and Tyler went to the pizza restaurant to talk to Alex's mom. It was good timing as Sonya had just finished serving one of the guests.

"Hey, boys. What are you up to this afternoon?"

"Mom, can you take us to the junkyard sometime? We've finished everything, but we still need to get the rails."

"I'm not working on Saturdays, so I think I'll be ok for Saturday morning," Sonya said. She was happy to see Alex with a nice group of friends.

"Thank you, Mrs. Mil-ler," Tyler was kind of singing in his "Mr. Nice Guy" voice.

Tuesday morning, at the coffee shop. Lankford was drinking his

---

cast, plaster protection for a broken bone
to flip, to turn upside down

usual cup of coffee. This morning he walked to his car with his coffee and his newspaper under his left arm. His right hand was always free to *grab* his gun if he had to. Lankford had already got into his seat and closed his door when he noticed his *rear view mirror* was *pointing upwards* so that he could not see the back seat. Almost immediately, he felt the gun in the back of his neck.

"Start the car and drive your normal route. I need to talk to you," Aaron *demanded* in a low voice. "Keep both hands on the steering wheel."

"Listen, now! It would be a very bad idea to jump out and signal someone for help. If you do, I'll have to visit your lovely wife and two children as well. I've been watching you for a couple of months," Aaron said. "I feel like I know you very well. By the way, I think it's really sweet the way your wife makes you a lunch pack every day."

They were driving towards the FBI office.

"So let's talk," said Lankford, he could hardly breathe.

"I need Danny Torbert's address. See? Nothing too *tricky*."

"I haven't had contact with them in over a year! They only contact me if they need me. I have no idea where they are," Lankford said.

"Tell me how to contact them." Aaron's voice was still quiet. "Give me phone numbers, e-mails, passwords, or anything you've set up to *communicate* with them."

Silence.

---

to grab, to reach for quickly
rear view mirror [ˈmɪrə], mirror in car for seeing behind
to point upwards, to point up in the air
to demand [dɪˈmɑːnd], to want
tricky, not easy
to communicate [kəˈmjuːnɪkeɪt], to talk or write to someone

"Oh, come on," Aaron said. "I've had *hackers* working on this since we found you. They'll soon get the information anyway, but I'm in a hurry, you see. Help me out and you will live. If not, the hackers will find the information anyway, and then you will have died for nothing. Save us all some trouble. Save yourself."

hacker, computer criminal

No, too many lives were at risk here – not just Danny's and Eileen's, Lankford thought to himself. He no longer missed the drug raids; he missed his family.

Lankford shook his head.

"Are you sure? What about your wife and kids?"

Aaron *pulled the trigger*, and then he shot. He opened the door and rolled onto the sidewalk as Lankford's car *smashed into* an *oncoming truck*.

Aaron brushed himself off as the blue Honda stopped to pick him up.

"Anything?" Frank asked.

"No. That was bad luck"

"Yeah, it looks like it!"

---

to pull the trigger, to fire the gun
to smash into, to crash into
oncoming, coming at you
truck [trʌk], lorry

The next morning in class, everything changed.

Two students handed out a copy of "USA Today" on each desk.

On the front page Alex saw a full color photo of the smashed cars. He almost stopped breathing when he read the *headline*: "FBI Officer Shot, Others Dead in Car Crash."

Like an explosion, the memories flashed in his brain. The gunshots. The falling body. The silent scream.

The eleven-year-old boy Danny Torbert was the real boy behind Alex and all the other *fake* identities. He used to live in Chicago. On weekends, he and his family would go to parks, ride bikes, and play board games. During the week, everyone was busy. Danny rode his bike to school. His mom Eileen worked at the bank. Rick, his dad, worked, but Danny had never been sure what his job was. His dad used to say he worked with computers if anybody asked.

Danny was always told to go to his room when his dad's work friends came to visit. But from what Danny could hear from his room it seemed that his dad worked with some sort of *surveillance* and not computers. Who was he watching? And why was that kept so secret?

Rick didn't like to bring work home, but when he had to, his *colleague*, Steve, was the one who came to visit the most.

---

headline ['hedlaɪn], leading line of a newspaper article
fake, false or not what it is supposed to be
surveillance [sə'veɪləns], secretly watching someone
colleague ['kɒliːg], person you work with

He was always friendly with Danny, and they would always give each other *high fives* before Danny was asked to go.

Once, just once, a tall, thin man came with Steve. That day, Rick got really angry. He ran to the door and wanted the guy to leave at once.

"I told you I don't want him in my house!" Rick shouted at Steve. Danny found out that the other man's name was Aaron. Danny had never seen his dad angry like that before.

The day it all happened started out perfectly well. There was a half day at school and his dad was going to take him to a new rock wall. Danny loved climbing and couldn't wait to get to the new wall. So when he saw Steve's car in the driveway, he got very disappointed.

Danny went around the back of the house so that he wouldn't make any noise.

As he opened the door he could hear them shouting at one another.

"I don't see why you're being such a *jerk* about this!" Steve shouted.

"Because the guy is guilty!" His dad shouted back. "We've been watching him for months. I heard some of the phone recordings from less than an hour ago!"

"So did I ... and so did the rest of the team!" Steve

---

jerk [dʒɜːk], idiot

answered back. "And we haven't heard anything to *prove* that he has a *connection* to terrorists!"

"But that's not true, Steve!" His dad was furious. "The *conversations* are perfectly clear. He talks about guns, money, dates, and times. This guy is working with terrorists! There is no question whatsoever!" Suddenly his dad got quiet. "Unless someone *altered* the tape ..." His dad's voice got louder. "Wait, I've got a copy of the tape right here."

Danny picked up the phone to call his mom – she would know what to do. Then he stopped. He got to think that he was *overreacting*, and that his dad was just having an *argument* with Steve.

Danny put down the phone.

"Let's listen to the rest of that tape!" His dad shouted again.

Danny could hear a recorded voice, but he couldn't hear the words.

"Right there!" his dad *roared*. "Did you hear that? He's buying weapons."

There was a pause, and then his dad roared again, "Did he just say your name? How could you do it, Steve? How could you *betray* your own country?" Rick shouted. "You're working for him, aren't you? You're selling him weapons and *covering* it *up*, aren't you?"

---

to prove [pruːv], to make clear
connection [kəˈnekʃən], link or association with
conversation [ˌkɒnvəˈseɪʃən], talking with someone
to alter [ˈɔːltə], to change
to overreact [ˌəʊvəriˈækt], to react too strongly
argument [ˈɑːgjumənt], a fight or a disagreement
to roar [rɔːr], to shout loudly
to betray [bɪˈtreɪ], to be disloyal to
to cover up, to hide the truth

Steve said nothing.

"You and who else? Frank? Aaron?" Rick shouted.

Danny couldn't take it anymore. He picked up the phone and called his mom's work number.

"Can I speak to Eileen Torbert, please?" he asked. When he got through to his mom's bank he was put on hold.

Suddenly Danny could hear the sounds of breaking glass and *furniture* flying through the air.

Why hadn't Mom answered his call yet? Danny ran to the office door and pushed it open.

Rick and Steve were fighting. Both stopped and stared at the boy.

"Dad? Are you okay?" Danny's voice *cracked*.

Steve was the first to move. He grabbed the phone and pressed the talk button. They could hear the music from the bank's *hold line*.

"Who did you call, Danny?" Steve screamed in Danny's face while he knocked Danny against the wall.

Rick screamed and threw the coffee table at Steve. The table sent Steve flying backwards to land on the floor. Rick punched Steve, again and again. Steve got free of Rick's punches; his face was all *swollen* and full of blood. Suddenly, as if in slow motion Danny watched Steve turn around to grab his gun. He pointed his gun at Rick. Then he fired. Over, and over, and over again. His father's body fell to the floor. He was dead.

Danny knew he screamed, but he couldn't hear his own scream because of the sound of Steve's gun.

---

furniture [ˈfɜːnɪtʃə], tables and chairs
to crack, to break
hold line, waiting line
swollen [ˈswəʊlən], made larger than normal

Danny knew what was next. He got to his feet.

Steve rolled to his side and fired again, but Danny was already out of the office. He ran through the kitchen and out of the back door. He got into the backyard, then he heard the gunshot and felt something hit his body.

He felt *weightless*. Then, he felt nothing.

Two weeks passed before Danny *regained consciousness*. And it wasn't until a month later that he could remember exactly what had happened.

He lost the *lower lobe* of his right *lung* and would need months, maybe years, of training to regain his strength.

Two weeks later a teacher came to teach Danny from home. He wasn't strong enough to go to school the next couple of months because of his *injury*. Danny also had to do a lot of training. He hated every minute of it. His body was very weak. His *mental* strength wasn't there at all. He just didn't care.

Danny hated group *counseling*. It was like being on "Oprah Winfrey's talk show." Get in touch with your feelings; set yourself free. He knew his feelings would not set him free. It was all his fault. He had waited too long to call his mom. If he had called his mom earlier, the police could have been there in time to save his dad. Instead, he had *burst into* the room with the phone in his hand. He had caused his

---

weightless [ˈweɪtləs], feeling like you are floating
to regain [rɪˈɡeɪn] *consciousness* [ˈkɒnʃəsnəs], to wake up after being hit on the head etc.
injury [ˈɪndʒəri], wound
mental, psychological
counseling [ˈkaʊnsəlɪŋ], advice given by a doctor, social worker etc.
to burst [bɜːst] *into*, to come suddenly into a room etc.

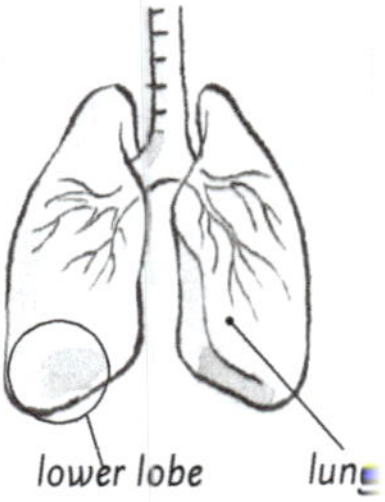

father's death and there was nothing Danny could do to bring him back. Danny believed that he was just as guilty as Steve.

One afternoon as everyone was leaving the counseling session, Jorge, one of the other *patients* tried to *stab* Danny. The police found out that Steve had got Jorge in there only to kill Danny. After a long interview, Jorge told the police where they could find Steve. Steve was then arrested and in *police custody* within an hour.

Danny was brought to another hospital many miles away. There, his mother and someone called Mr. Lankford from the FBI talked to him in private.

Mr. Lankford explained that Danny was *in danger* because he was a witness to Steve's crime. The FBI wanted Danny and Eileen to *testify* against Steve in *court*. Mr. Lankford explained that Danny would have to tell the court about everything he knew and everything he had seen that day.

The *trial* was quick. Eileen explained that she had heard everything through the connection to Danny's phone. Mr. Lankford gave background information and said that the FBI *suspected* Steve of terrorist activities. Unfortunately there was not enough proof for that as Steve had destroyed all of the surveillance files. Steve was only *convicted* on the *charge of murder*, and not on the charges of terrorism. He was sentenced to life in prison.

---

patient [ˈpeɪʃənt], person in hospital
to stab, to wound with a knife
to be in police custody [ˈkʌstədi], to be put in a cell at the police station
to be in danger [ˈdeɪndʒə], to be in trouble or at risk
to testify [ˈtestɪfaɪ], to give evidence in a *court* of law
court [kɔːt], place where criminal *trials* take place
trial [ˈtraɪəl], event in court where the evidence is heard
to suspect [səˈspekt], to think that somebody is guilty of a crime
to be convicted [kənˈvɪktɪd], to be found guilty
charge of murder, accusation of having killed somebody

Lankford gave mother and son information about new identities, new lives, and new beginnings. That's how Danny and Eileen became Dylan and Nicole in Colorado. Then, they were Zack and Kate in Tennessee. Mr. Lankford gave Eileen a computer and taught her how she could create their identities herself. That way, she would only have to contact him if absolutely necessary.

As Danny – now Alex – stared at the article he could feel the guilt coming back to him. He now felt he had killed Mr. Lankford too.

CHAPTER 13

"Alex," Tim whispered. "What's wrong?"

Alex was standing, and everyone was staring at him. "I, uh …" He couldn't say a word.

"Mr. O'Neil, Alex feels sick. Can I get him to the *nurse*?"

"Yes, of course. Alex, are you ok? I'll call the nurse and tell her you're on the way."

Tim got Alex into the nearest bathroom.

"You have to tell me what's going on, Alex?" Tim waited, but got no answer. "Does this have something to do with the dead *cop*?"

Alex didn't move. He was trying to make the cold sweat go away.

"I'm your friend. You can talk to me." Tim continued. "Are you in some kind of trouble? Is that why you get quiet sometimes and act funny?"

Alex tried to look at his friend but had to drop his head again not to *throw up*.

"What can I do to help you?" Tim sounded worried.

Alex spoke with his head down the toilet, "Nothing, I'll be all right."

"Nothing? How can you say that? Dude, I'm your friend."

"Yeah, and I want to keep it that way. So just stay out of it and don't *mention* this to anyone, ok?"

"Stay out? I'm already in this."

---

nurse [nɜːs], doctor's helper
cop, slang for policeman
to throw [θrəʊ] *up* - *threw* [θruː], to get sick or vomit
to mention [ˈmenʃən], to say something without giving it much importance

"No you're not. So leave it alone, or you'll be dead too."

Tim was silent.

"I can't tell you anything," Alex said.

"You've got to stop running sometime!" Tim was shouting now. "I'd like to think that your friends here are important enough for you to make this your home."

Alex made eye contact with Tim. "My friends are important that's why I don't want them dead."

A second later, the nurse opened the door and saw Alex lying on the floor.

Alex looked Tim in the eye as if to say: Please, Tim. Help me.

"He couldn't make it down the hall. We came in here to get some water on his face." Tim explained to the nurse. Tim kept to Alex's side.

"Sonya, phone for you!" Bonnie shouted from the back of the pizza shop. Sonya almost dropped the cheese soup she was about to *serve*. A million thoughts went through her brain: What's wrong? No one knows I'm here, except … Alex!

"Hello? This is Sonya."

"Hi. This is Mrs. Layton, the school nurse. I'm afraid Alex is sick. He's all cold and sweaty. Can you come pick him up?"

"Oh, thank God!"

"Excuse me?"

"Oh, I mean, yes. I'll be right there."

Ed worked in the world's largest surveillance center, Echelon. Here the United States, Canada, Australia, New Zealand, and England worked together to check all e-mails, faxes, phone

---

to serve [sɜːv], here: to give something to somebody in a shop, restaurant etc.

calls, and text messages for *threatening* information. He was a *brilliant* hacker and used his *talent* to earn some extra money by working for Frank.

A week ago, Frank gave him another job: find all contacts *associated with* Tom Lankford of the FBI. It usually didn't take Ed long to trace messages back to the exact computer, phone, or *device* it had come from.

Ed started with Lankford's *workstation*, followed all incoming and outgoing messages to their servers, and *located* every workstation at the other end.

On Wednesday at 11:18 a.m., while Alex was lying in the nurse's office, Ed made the important phone call.

"Frank, I've got the addresses. Now you bring the money."

---

threatening ['θretənɪŋ], warning or promising danger
brilliant ['brɪljənt], very clever
talent ['tælənt], ability to do something very well
to be associated [ə'səʊsieɪtɪd] *with*, to be connected to
device [dɪ'vaɪs], electronic item like a mobile phone
workstation, here: computer and telephone
to locate [ləʊ'keɪt], to find

Chapter 14

"Mom, Mr. Lankford is dead."

They were both sitting in the car about to leave the school.

"What?"

"It was in this morning's newspaper. They shot him!" Alex screamed. In the last couple of years, his mother had never seen her son lose control. But now, he was completely *freaked out*. "They know! We're in trouble! We have to leave! We..."

"Ok, just a minute," his mom cut in. "How do we know it was Steve?"

"Because, I can feel it."

"Ok. First I need to see this newspaper. Let's see exactly what it says before we go crazy."

"Crazy? We've moved for a lot less than this," Alex was crying.

They were both silent as they drove home. They didn't speak again until they were inside their own house.

"Ok," his mom continued once the door was closed. "Just think about this for a minute. Even if they did kill him, he didn't tell them anything ... He didn't know anything. The only communication I've had with him in the last two years has been through e-mail. And I stopped doing that at least two moves ago. Nobody knows where we are."

"Still, Lankford is dead – murdered and we're left waiting for somebody to find us," Alex said quietly.

"No, we've taken control of our own lives. As long as we don't do anything to *attract attention* to ourselves, we're as

---

to freak [friːk] out, to go crazy
to attract [əˈtrækt] *attention*, to try to get people to look in your direction

safe as we've always been."

"I guess you're right. I'm sorry I freaked out."

"You don't really want to leave here, do you?"

"No. I like this place."

"I can tell," she smiled. "I like it too. Let's stay for right now. But let's be sure to keep our eyes open."

"So what exactly does this mean?" Steve was holding information from Lankford's computer in his hand. "It means that we know where Eileen was when she last contacted Lankford."

"I don't care about that," Steve *snapped*. "At least not yet, my appeal date is less than two months away."

"I understand."

"Good. So where are they **now**?"

"We don't know. We're hoping Eileen tries to contact Lankford's office when she sees the headlines."

Steve couldn't believe his ears. He was *furious*. "Let me get this straight. You try to get the information from Lankford, but you can't so you kill him. Then I pay some computer guy $200,000 to do all this paperwork, and we still don't know where they are?"

"No, but there's the…"

"Shut up!" Steve suddenly said. He was looking at the *security guard*, who was now walking towards them. The guard gave them a *warning* look and walked back to his post. Steve continued more quietly. "I'm not waiting for her to contact

---

to snap, to speak sharply
to be furious ['fʊəriəs], to be very angry
security [sɪ'kjʊərəti] *guard*, private 'policeman'
warning, notice of coming danger

them. She hasn't contacted them for over a year, and she would be stupid to do it now."

Frank nodded in agreement.

"Where are the girls?" Steve continued.

"They've just finished with Maryland."

"This is going way too slow." Steve leaned in closer to Frank. "It's time to do something different. Use your *government* contacts to get into the social security files. I mean, if Eileen began working in November or December, the social security office would have a new number to show us in that state. Look for a single parent with a child at a nearby school."

"But there's millions...and we don't know which state."

"Then you shouldn't be wasting your time talking to me." Steve leaned back in his chair. The conversation was over.

Frank walked out of the room. He could feel Steve's eyes burning a hole in his back.

---

government ['gʌvənmənt], the elected leaders of a country

Chapter 15

For a week and a half, Alex *pretended* that everything was ok. He wanted to be the good son and let his mom believe he was fine.

But for some reason he knew something was wrong. He would have to be prepared to run away any moment.

To make them feel safer, his mom bought two new mobile phones for emergencies only.

"You have to go on as if nothing happened. If you start acting *paranoid*, you'll attract attention," his mom reminded him.

That Saturday, Sonya drove the boys to the junkyard to search for a rail. After an hour of *searching*, they found an old, eight-foot long, steel pipe. Tim politely thanked Alex's mom, but didn't say a word to Alex. Alex was wondering what was wrong with Tim, but he also decided not to *bother* too much. After all he had promised his mom not to be too paranoid.

They met all week after school to practice. Tim's mom basically had to *drag* them *off* the ramp each night after dark.

One Friday night, Tim, Tyler, and Nate agreed to meet after breakfast the next morning. Alex, however, had to *cancel*: "I can't come tomorrow. Will you guys be here on Sunday?"

Tim gave him a look.

---

to pretend [pri'tend], to act in a false way
to be paranoid ['pærənɔɪd], to feel that someone is after you
to search [sɜːtʃ], to look for
to bother ['bɒðə], to worry
to drag off, to pull away
to cancel ['kænsəl], to say that you cannot come anyway

"What are you doing?" Tyler then asked.

"There's something I got to do with my mom." Alex said.

"We'll be here Sunday," Nate said as he was getting on his bike. "See you guys tomorrow."

"Wait," Tyler shouted trying to catch up with Nate.

Tim looked at Alex when the other two were away. "Will you really be here on Sunday?"

Alex understood his meaning. "I'm not leaving, Tim. There's just something I've got to do tomorrow."

"What?"

"What do you mean, 'what'?"

"I mean," Tim said, "what are you doing tomorrow?"

"I told you, I'm going somewhere with my mom," Alex said.

"Why do you always have to be like this?"

"Like what?"

"Like this!" Tim said much louder. "You give me a lot of half answers all the time. You don't even mention that day at school when you freaked. What's going on with you?"

"Nothing's going on," Alex *assured*. "I just freaked that day at school. But I think I've got it worked out. I'll be here Sunday, don't worry."

Tim nodded. After a moment, he said, "You know if you need my help just tell me..."

"Yeah, I know." Alex looked down. "I hope it doesn't come to that ... Thanks though. I'll see you Sunday, Tim."

Gina walked down the steps of Pocomoke High School. They finished their search in Maryland and were moving on to

---

to assure [əˈʃʊə], to say that you are certain or confident that a fact is true work through the state of Virginia on Monday. Danny wasn't in Maryland, and there was no way Eileen would send him to school in one state and work in another, Gina thought to herself. She wouldn't be close enough if something happened.

Gina was getting worried. Some of their other clients in the Midwest were getting *impatient*. Aaron was in Minnesota now, to see some of the customers, but he needed help. Gina and Leah should be helping Aaron, not wasting their time looking for the boy and his mom. Steve was *ruining* their business by all his demands.

It was time to *get rid of* Steve. Aaron could take his place, no problem. Gina knew she wouldn't make a good leader herself. She didn't mind killing people, but she was too *hot-headed* to be in charge. However, Aaron was smart and *ruthless*. He would do whatever it took to get the job done.

If they didn't find the kid by the time they covered South Carolina, she would have to talk to Frank and Aaron about getting rid of Steve.

There were over fifteen high schools in the Norfolk and Virginia Beach area alone. That really was too much time wasted!

She wanted to kill someone right now.

---

to be impatient [ɪm'peɪʃnt], to be restless or not willing to wait
to ruin [ru:ɪn] to destroy or spoil
to get rid of, to destroy, kill or throw away
to be hot-headed, to get angry quickly
to be ruthless [ru:θləs], to be cruel or mean

Chapter 16

On Saturday, Sonya and Alex made a short trip away from town. When Alex got out of the car he could see nothing but trees. Some of the trees even had blue and red paint *splattered* on them.

"Have a good time, honey."

"I will," Alex said, looking around to see if anyone heard. Mom should know not to call him honey when there could be other kids around.

"Call me when you're ready."

"I will." He shut the door and gave her a wave as she turned the car around and slowly left the driveway.

Then he saw Brian walking up behind him.

"I'm glad you found the place," Brian said.

The boys rode four-wheelers through the woods for two full hours.

"Wow! That was cool!" Alex said when they were back in the house.

"Yeah, I thought you'd like it," Brian said with the first real smile Alex had seen him show.

"Hey, do your parents own all these woods?"

"My dad does. My mom lives in Pittsburgh. There's thirty-two *acres* – Dad likes his *privacy.*"

"That's for sure. I couldn't hear a thing – no cars, no *sirens*, nothing."

---

to splatter, to splash
acre [ˈeɪkə], a measure of land (4047 square metres)
privacy [ˈprɪvəsi], your own private place
siren [ˈsaɪrən], noise from a police car or ambulance

"Yeah, it's quiet. You want lunch?"

"Definitely," said Alex.

The kitchen showed very well that Brian's mom didn't live there. Things were clean, but messy. There were no flowers on the table and the plates had Harley Davidson logos on them. Alex missed the typical 'man' stuff in his own home.

"The bathroom is the second door on your right if you want a wash."

Alex looked down at his *muddy* hands. That made him smile. "Ok, thanks," he said. "I think that would be a good idea."

Alex noticed a small, gray box beside the phone on his way down the hall. *Weird,* he said to himself.

Brian's dad came in a little bit later for lunch. He was a tall, heavy man with his clothes covered in oil. "Hi," he said. "You must be Alex. I'm Brian's dad but you can call me Ron. Sorry about the oil," he smiled and was pointing at his clothes.

Brian stared at his dad, "I thought you were going to be working on your truck," he said.

"I am working on the truck, son. I just came in to get something to eat."

Alex tried to break the *tension.* "Hi, Ron," he said, "what a lovely place you have. I love the woods being all around you."

"Thanks. I like space, and I don't have to worry about my neighbors," Ron smiled.

Alex smiled back: "Thanks for letting me come over. I really like the four-wheelers." He was still looking around the room.

---

muddy ['mʌdi], dirty
weird ['wɪəd], strange
tension ['tenʃən], uncomfortable situation

Then he saw the box on Ron's *ankle.*

"Yeah, Brian and I race them all the time. He has learned how to fix them too," Ron said.

Brian left for the bathroom.

Then Ron whispered, "I'm really glad you came. Brian has been talking about you since you moved here. You've really made an *impression* on him."

"Uh, thanks," Alex said quietly.

"No, I mean it. Ever since you *stood up* for him, he's been a different person. And I wanted you to know I *appreciate* it."

---

to make an impression, to make someone pay attention
to stand up for, to back up
to appreciate [ə'pri:ʃieɪt], to be happy about something

When Brian came back Ron changed back to talk about racing four-wheelers.

After lunch, Brian wanted them to go back to the garage. "I've got something else to show you," he said.

Brian took Alex to a large *cabinet*. He opened the doors and there in the cabinet were a lot of guns.

"Guns? Are these yours?" Alex asked. He couldn't help it - guns made him nervous.

"Yep! They're all paintball guns. They are really cool!"

Alex smiled. "So you run around the woods and shoot trees?"

"No, I use the trees for practice. Do you want to try?" Brian asked.

All Alex really wanted to say was, "No thanks. This is a little too real-life for me." But instead, he said, "Oh, yeah, that would be great."

Brian handed him *padded camouflaged clothes* and a *face mask*.

"Is all this necessary?" Alex asked.

"Yeah, the balls sting really badly if you are not *protected*."

Brian taught Alex the basics. Then they spent the next hour or so shooting after each other through the woods. Brian was an excellent shot.

When Brian went in the house later to get two cans of coke, Ron came back to talk.

"I want to thank you again for all you've done for Brian," Ron said.

---

cabinet, closet or place for hanging clothes
padded camouflage ['kæməflɑːʒ] *clothes*, see illustration p. 60
face mask, see illustration p. 60
to protect [prə'tekt], to wear special clothes that prevent injury

"It's ok," Alex said with a smile. "I really didn't do anything that I wouldn't have done for anyone else."

"Yeah, but even those losers he usually hangs around with didn't try to help him with the firecracker thing," Ron continued. He caught Alex looking at the box on his leg. "Are you wondering about this thing around my ankle?"

Alex's face went red.

Ron showed Alex the black band and small silver on his ankle. "I was drinking one night after work, and I decided to drive home. The most stupid thing I've ever done. I hit a girl who tried to run across the road."

Alex nodded.

"I got ten years. They let me out after three, and I'm under *house arrest* for two years. I can go to work, to the shop, and home. Anything else, I have to call the police and

---

house arrest [ə'rest], police order to stay at home

get *permission* first. If I step out of these woods without calling them, I'll go back to jail."

"Dad!" Brian shouted as he walked in. "You shouldn't tell my friends things like that!" You could see that Brian was really embarrassed.

"Brian, really, don't worry about it," Alex said with a friendly smile.

"This is all I need. My dad's going around telling my friends he's a *convict*."

"Dude, it's okay. People make mistakes. I'm not going to tell anybody."

"Don't you get it?" Brian asked. "If people find out he's been in jail, people will ... I might as well move!"

"Look, Brian, at least you have a dad."

The words were out of Alex's mouth before he could stop it.

Brian looked shocked!

"I'm sorry, Brian, that just came out. Uh ... wow ... My dad ... died ... a few years ago, and I've been thinking a lot about him ... And ..." Alex continued, "I'm sorry ... And if you feel sorry for me, I'll kill you."

Brian smiled at Alex's joke. "Ok then - I'm really sorry about your dad, Alex."

"Yeah," Alex whispered. "Um look, I really don't like to talk about that, so if you could ... just ... not tell anybody that I told you..."

"I won't," Brian said. "And you won't tell anybody about anything here, right?"

"*Deal*," Alex agreed.

---

to get permission [pəˈmɪʃən], to be allowed to do something
convict [ˈkɒnvɪkt], person in jail
deal [diːl], agreement

Ed was sure that Frank was Satan. He could remember his grandmother telling him, "Boy, if you want to make a deal with the devil, you'll get burned." She was so right.

Ed had set up an account with a little bank in the Philippines. He wanted to move there as soon as the money from Frank was *transferred* to his account. But for now, he had to work hard. If he didn't do what he was told Frank would come after him as usual. Frank and a tall, thin guy seemed to be everywhere just to check him out. Ed had sold his soul.

Ed checked one social security code after the other. He had found just over thirty single parents with only one child who were new to Virginia in November.

He would call Satan later and tell him about his result so far.

"Right, Brian, well done!" Miss Jenkins was very happy with all the answers Brian could give her even on difficult questions.

Yes, go Brian! Alex thought. Maybe Brian's dad was right. Brian did seem like a different person.

"What's up with Brian?" Tim whispered. "Did he eat a *science book* for breakfast?"

Alex smiled. "Maybe he couldn't find anybody's lunch to steal."

Tim smiled, but he had also noticed that Brian hadn't been punching the younger kids all week. Something was up.

---

to transfer [træns'fɜː], to send
science ['saɪəns] *book*, schoolbook for a subject like biology

"I was wondering if you could help me Mrs. Wisniewski. I'm trying to make a survey on new students here in the Virginia area," Gina lied. "Today I have already interviewed three girls and five African American students. Do you have any white American boy by any chance that has started school this month?"

"Yes, I actually do," Mrs. Wisniewski said. She was happy to show Gina the information on her computer screen.

"There you go. Alex Miller from Michigan."

"Thank you." Gina smiled. "I think he'll be perfect."

Chapter 18

Mrs. Wisniewski called Miss Jenkins.

"Could you send Alex Miller to the office, please?"

Alex's heart stopped beating. What could they possibly want? Maybe his mom was on the phone. Maybe she was hurt. No. They would come to the door and ask for him quietly then. Maybe they found out he was not Alex. Maybe...

"Sure, he's on his way. Alex, leave your books, and bring your *hall-pass* with you," Miss Jenkins said.

Alex looked around the hallway for anything strange. He could feel every *hair on his neck rising.*

When he got to the office Mrs. Wisniewski was talking on the phone and writing something down on paper.

A tall lady with dark hair sat in a chair to his right. She had a notebook and a nice pen in front of her.

"Alex," Mrs. Wisniewski said as she put down the phone. "Miss Reynolds is here from the Department of Education. She is interviewing new students in the state to see how our schools meet their various needs. We selected you *at random* to answer a survey."

Alex didn't like this at all. Selected? Survey? Interview? He liked the word random though, that made him relax a little bit.

"Hi, Alex, I know you want to get back to class as soon as possible." Gina smiled.

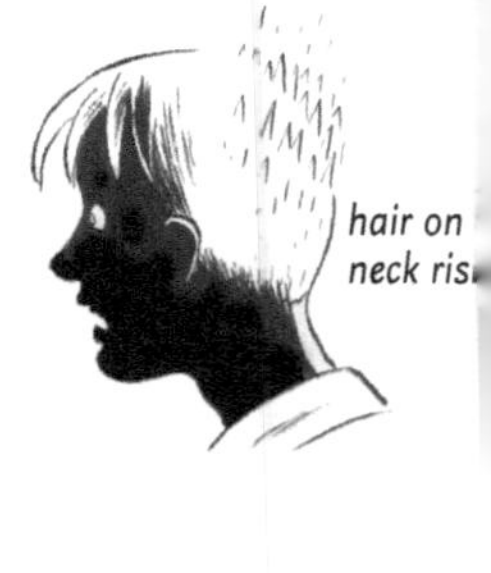

hall – pass, permit to leave the classroom
at random [ˈrændəm], with no pattern

"I just have a few questions, and I'll be out of your way."

He nodded. That sounded ok, but did she seem a little *anxious*, or was he being paranoid?

"Ok, first of all," Gina said, "I want to thank you for your help. This is an *anonymous* survey, so your name won't be *registered* in any way."

Alex couldn't help it, he felt suspicious. She was really looking him over, wasn't she? He tried to look her in the eye, but she was busy looking at his hair, his ears, and his chin. He also felt she was looking to see if he had any scars on his chest. When she finally made eye contact with him, she knew she was being caught.

"Where did you move from?"

"Michigan." Alex said. *Get a grip*, he told himself. He was speaking too quickly and showing that he was nervous.

"Were your classes in Michigan (a) easier, (b) more *challenging*, or (c) about the same?"

"About the same," he answered. It seemed as good an answer as any.

"What level math did you take at your former school...?" She asked him a lot more questions about his old school and his move here. She asked the questions very quickly. Then *without warning* she closed her notebook and thanked Alex for his time. She left the room, thanked the secretary, and walked out of the building.

---

to be anxious [ˈæŋkʃəs], to be worried
anonymous [əˈnɒnɪməs], not giving any names
to register [ˈredʒɪstə], to record
to get a grip, to get control of yourself
challenging [ˈtʃælɪndʒɪŋ], hard to do
without warning, suddenly

Alex looked at Mrs. Wisniewski. "Is that all she does? Surveys?"

"I guess so," the secretary answered. "You'd be surprised what they pay people to do."

Alex watched as Gina left the school area. She was driving rather quickly for someone who was driving in an area filled with children. The whole situation felt wrong. Paranoid or not, he needed to get out of here.

"Mrs. Wisniewski, can I use your phone, Alex asked the secretary.

"Is it an emergency, Alex?"

"Yes. I think that woman who was just here is part of a *plot* to hunt me down and kill me," Alex thought to himself. But instead he said: "No, but my mom would like to know I've just been interviewed without her permission."

"Well, then tell her tonight and ask her to call us if there's a problem," Mrs. Wisniewski just said. "Give me your pass, and I'll sign you back into class."

He handed her his pass. He had to get out of there as quickly as possible.

As soon as Gina was *out of eyesight*, she pulled over to one side. She was all excited. She found Frank's mobile number: "Frank? I've got him."

---

plot, a plan (often secret or dangerous)
out of eyesight ['aɪsaɪt], where you cannot be seen

Alex looked around for an easy exit. He checked the time. It was 11:48. In two minutes, his class would be *dismissed* and the halls would be full of students … and teachers. He would have to time this just right.

He wrote a note and put it in his pocket.

As he got to his class, the bell rang. The doors flew open and students were everywhere. Then he saw Tim.

He quickly handed him his note. "You didn't see me come back, ok?" Alex whispered.

Tim's eyes grew round as he understood. Tim handed Alex his bag. He took out his sweatshirt and his phone and gave the bag back to Tim.

"Can you hold this for me?" Alex asked his friend, but he didn't wait for an answer.

Alex disappeared. He was keeping his head low so that he wouldn't make eye contact with any of the teachers.

Tim opened the note and read:

Tim,
I hope you meant what you said, because I think they found me.
Please go home after school; I'll try to call you there.
Don't tell anyone. I hope I'm wrong.

Alex

---

to dismiss [dɪs'mɪs], to send away

Alex walked out of one of the side doors next to the *foreign language* hallway. He just needed to make it to his bike.

He slid along the school wall, below the windows, as quickly as he could. When he got to the fire exit doors, he had to stop and check for teachers. The coast was clear.

He jumped on his bike. He knew that there was no way he was going to get out of the school playground *unnoticed,* but there was no choice.

"We just landed in Chicago, but we can be on another plane within the hour," Frank told Gina on his mobile phone. "The plane to Virginia Beach Airport will take another three hours. We'll call you as soon as we land. Are you sure it's him?"

"I'm not one hundred percent sure," Gina said. "But I've *studied* his picture *very closely*. The eyes, chin, and smile all match. Also he was quite nervous, like he had something to hide. I really think it's him."

"We'll let Ed keep working through the data files until we're a hundred percent sure. E-mail me if there's a problem. Whatever you do, don't lose him."

"I got his address off the computer screen when the secretary showed me his picture," Gina said. "When he gets home, we'll walk in and grab both of them."

"Fantastic, but watch the school anyway. We can't let him escape like he did in Colorado."

"I'm already *in position,*" she assured him and pushed the

---

foreign ['fɒrɪn] *language*, any language other than your own
to be unnoticed, without being seen
to study very closely, to look at very carefully
in position, in place and ready for action

end' button on her mobile phone. Now all she had to do was wait. In five hours, this would all be over and she could go home and relax in time for the weekend. That very minute she saw Danny coming out of the school playground on his bike, he got across two lanes of traffic, and down a side street before she could even move.

"That little punk!" Gina shouted as she started her car and pulled into traffic. He was not going to ruin another weekend.

Chapter 20

Alex rode as fast as he could down the street. He just wanted to put some *distance* between himself and the school.

He turned onto a side street and pulled over to call his mom. However, he didn't have a chance to get the phone out of his pocket before he could hear a very fast car behind him. He looked over his shoulder to see the white car speeding by. The driver was the woman he had just met at school. Their eyes met for a second then she hit the *brakes* and turned the car around.

Alex rode like a madman. He cut through someone's yard and rode across the *lawn*, through another yard, and onto a parallel street. He could hear the car changing gear and turning the corner.

He quickly got across the next yard before she could see him. He stopped next to a *shed* and dropped flat on the ground. He had to wait and see where she was going.

When she realized she had lost him, Gina was *swearing* out loudly to herself.

She pulled her car off to the side of the road. He couldn't be far away. She had been chasing him for about fifteen minutes. He had to be tired. All she could do was to wait and listen.

shed

distance, amount of length (e.g. 100 metres)
brake, pedal for stopping a car
lawn [lɔːn], see illustration p. 71
to swear [sweə], to say bad words

"Hey you! What are you doing in my yard?" An old woman was shouting at Alex, and Gina knew she had found him.

"*Gotcha,*" Gina said and turned the key.

Alex got back on his feet and ran the bike to the next street. As he jumped on the bike, he could hear the car turning the corner. He hoped he could hold on for just a few more minutes.

He decided to try his trick again. He knew his body was not going to last for much more.

As the car got closer, he knew she wanted to run him over. He got into the next driveway just in time to see the car pass by him onto the sidewalk and into a *lamppost.*

He drove up the long driveway and looked back to see Gina get out of her *wrecked* car. He smiled and then he panicked as he found out that he was trapped in a *fenced-in* backyard.

"You're mine, little *brat!*" she shouted. Gina didn't give up.

---

gotcha, slang for got you
to wreck [rek], to destroy
fenced-in, closed in on all sides
brat, slang for child

She grabbed the 9 mm gun from under her seat.

This was her prize for all the trouble this kid had caused. She had it planned: one in the head and two in the chest. She would take no chances.

She got to the end of the driveway only to see a beautiful swimming pool, but no Danny.

Danny heard the click, click, click of Gina's heels coming up the cement. He had to get over the fence.

He climbed as fast as he could; he hardly felt the blood dripping from his hands. He quickly and quietly climbed down on the other side.

For a few minutes he ran through the trees, crossed two roads, and then he had to slow down. He was too exhausted. But there was no time for a rest; he had to call his mom. She was in danger, too.

Gina checked all the doors but they were all locked. Then, she saw a bit of blood on the fence. That little punk got away, she thought. But he's hurt.

She took off her shoes and ran back to her car. She had to get out of there before the cops turned up. A few people were coming out of their houses to see what all this was about.

Too many witnesses! She needed a lift to get away. She smiled to them all, and then a nicely dressed man asked her if she was ok.

She covered her head and faked that she was *confused*. "I

---

to be confused [kən'fju:zd], to mix up things (in your head) think I have a *concussion*. Some kid tried to *carjack* me. Can you get me to a doctor?"

He helped her into his Audi and drove her down the sideway towards town. She relaxed and enjoyed the lift for a couple of minutes. She would wait until they were a few more miles away before she would kill this man. She had no choice; the man was now a witness.

---

concussion [kən'kʌʃən], injury to the head
carjack ['kɑːdʒæk], stealing a car

CHAPTER 21

Gina had informed Frank that she now had another car and was on her way to Danny's house. It was bad news that Danny had escaped. On the other hand, Frank was glad that the boy was trying to run away, that made it clear that he was the kid they were looking for.

They had left Ed alive, as a backup. This meant that once they had killed Danny, Frank would have to fly back and kill Ed. He simply knew too much.

Alex looked at his hand. He had cut his thumb on his right hand and his left hand hurt like mad, he hoped it wasn't *sprained.* He used his t-shirt to make a *bandage* for his hand. He couldn't walk around bleeding all over the place.

Time to call his mom.

When the phone rang Sonya knew something was wrong. Alex had never used his new mobile before.

"Mom, they've found us. We've got to leave."

"WHAT? What happened? Are you okay? Where are you?"

"They found me at school." His voice was desperate. "Some lady was taking a survey and I got suspicious. She's chasing me through town."

"Are you okay?"

"Yeah, I cut my hand, but I'll be all right.

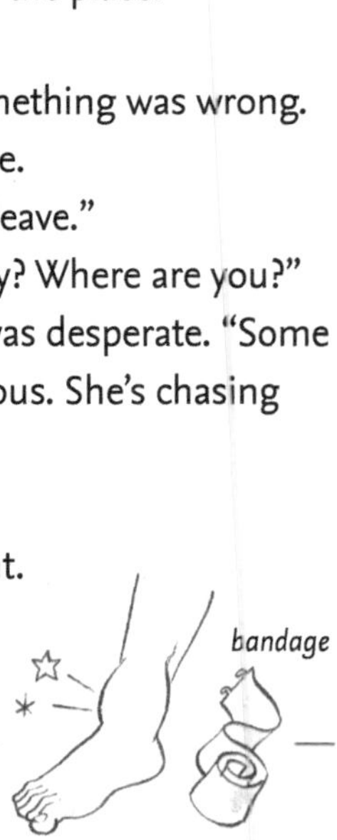

to sprain [spreɪn] *something,* to injure but not break e.g. your ankle

Can you come and get me? We've got to leave – now."

"Where are you?"

"I must be very close to the Great Neck shopping area. Do you want to meet outside the big supermarket there?"

"Good idea. But I have to stop by the house to get some money.

"Forget it, mom. I'm sure they already know where we live."

"I'll be careful. We won't make it too far without money Alex."

"Ok, but don't get anything else. We really have to get out of here!"

"I'll be there within fifteen minutes."

Six minutes later, his mother got to their driveway. She saw no unusual cars or people hanging around. She turned off her car. "Just get the money and leave," she said to herself. She opened the car door and walked up the sidewalk. She tried to see into her house as she walked but then she remembered that she always kept the curtains closed. She now turned the key and unlocked the front door. She was *relieved*, no one was there. Wasting no time, she went into the bedroom and grabbed her old shoe box with the money and social security numbers – her 'running box' as she called it.

She hardly felt Gina's gun hit the back of her head.

---

relieved [rɪˈliːvd], happy that something bad has not happened

Gina wrote a text message: "I've got Eileen" and sent it off to Frank. She had tied Eileen up and with difficulty pulled her into the *trunk* of the Audi.

"Good," Frank replied. "Make sure you keep her there for the next two hours until we get there. If Danny shows up, try not to kill him yet. Aaron is looking forward to doing that."

"What if he decides to run?" she wrote back.

"He won't leave without his mother. He'll call soon, don't worry. Give him these directions."

Alex arrived at the supermarket ten minutes after his phone call. He went to the bathroom to wash his hands and his face. The bleeding had just about stopped on his right hand, so he took off his bandage – it drew too much attention.

He bought a Pepsi so that he wouldn't look too suspicious. Then he went back outside.

It had been fourteen minutes since the call.

Three minutes later, he started getting really worried. He found a good place where he could overlook the whole parking area. Then he sat down and waited.

Twenty minutes later he knew his mom wasn't coming. She would have called if she was *delayed*. Now should he

---

trunk [trʌŋk], compartment in the back of the car
to be delayed [dɪˈleɪd], to be late

take the risk and call, or wait until he heard something. No, he had to know.

He dialed the number. The phone at the other end rang twice.

"Hello?" It was a *female* voice, but not his mom's.

"I need to speak to Sonya."

"Well, Danny," the voice said. "This **is** Danny, right?"

His worst fear had come true. They had his mom. He should have tried harder to convince her not to go home. He should have known better. He did know better, but he let her go anyway. She was either dead or close to it, and it was his fault. Again.

"I'll take that as a 'yes'," the female voice continued. "You see, your mom can't talk to you right now, she's in the trunk of my car."

"Is she alive?"

"Yeah, she's alive, but not for much longer if I don't see you, Danny." He could hear her smiling through the phone.

"Do you want me to believe that you'll let her go if I show up," Danny said *sarcastically*.

She continued, "Well, she has a better chance of living with you here, than she does without you. Are you willing to take that chance?"

Danny said nothing. Of course he was willing to take that chance. He had to do everything he could to save her. Even though he knew it was a *trap*.

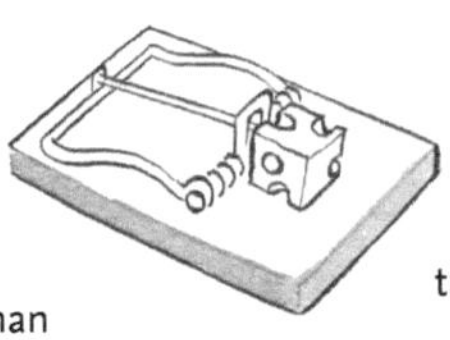
trap

to take the risk, to take a chance
female [ˈfiːmeɪl] voice, voice of a girl or a woman
sarcastically [sɑːˈkæstɪkli], with bitter comment

"Now, you just bring yourself home and we'll handle this quietly."

She was still at his house! Although he was stupid enough to get into this situation to begin with, Danny was smart enough not to go home. He had seen enough movies to know that situations like these should take place in public. There was less chance that she would shoot him with a lot of witnesses around. "No," he said.

"What?" She asked, not believing her ears. "Maybe I should just take care of things now."

"Let me talk to her," Danny demanded.

"Ooooh," she returned. "Has someone been watching crime shows on TV? Sure, you can talk to her."

Danny heard the *tape* being pulled off his mom's mouth.

"Alex?" it was his mom's voice.

"Mom!" He wanted to say he was sorry. He wanted to say that he would save her life if he could. He just wanted to talk to her.

He didn't get the chance.

"Ok, that's it!" said the female voice.

Danny heard a slapping sound. He hoped it was only the sound of tape being put back on his mom's mouth. Then he heard the sound of the trunk being slammed shut again.

"That's all you get, Danny. I think it's sweet how she still calls you Alex," the voice said sarcastically. "So are you coming or what?"

"You've got her locked in the trunk?" Danny shouted.

"She'll be all right as long as you show up." Gina said. "Well, what's your plan?"

He had to go, but that would be *suicide.* He needed a safe place. "I won't come there," he *stammered.* "It has to be somewhere public."

"There's that TV show again, Danny. Where would you like to meet?"

Good question, he thought. "We need to meet on the boardwalk."

"Hmmm. I don't know. I'll have to call you back about that. Oh and Danny by the way, I'm out of here as soon as I hang up, so don't bother to call the police. If you do, you know what will happen." The line went dead.

That was stupid. How was he going to get to the boardwalk? He should have told her to meet at a parking area. No, too many parked cars. There could be *a sniper* in any of them.

A sniper? Danny had an idea.

Five minutes later, Danny's phone rang. He answered on the first ring.

"Hello?"

"Danny." The female voice sounded *cheerful* – too cheerful. Something was up.

We'll meet at the golf course near the beach at 5:15."

"That's not on the boardwalk," Danny said angrily.

"Tough. You didn't think I would let you *dictate the terms,*

---

suicide ['suːɪsaɪd], the act of killing oneself
to stammer, to find it hard to speak
sniper ['snaɪpə], hidden gunman
cheerful ['tʃɪəfəl], happy
to dictate [dɪk'teɪt] *the terms,* to decide what's going to happen

did you?" she said with an ice-cold voice. "Here's the deal: You'll be standing alone at the golf course. We'll drive up and you'll get in. Your mom will be in a different car, so if you do something stupid like call the cops, that's it, then we will kill her."

"I'll need to talk to her before I get in any car."

"That's fine with me, Danny boy. And don't be stupid." She hung up.

Chapter 23

Danny needed time to think. As he walked toward the beach, he tried to make all of his ideas into a good plan. There had to be a way out of this mess. Calling the police was not a good idea, then they would kill his mom. What had he been thinking? The beach on a cold February afternoon was not going to be very busy at all. It would be getting dark by 5:15. Could he use the darkness to his *advantage*? Were Steve's men planning on doing the same thing?

He checked his mobile it was. 3:08. He dialed Tim's number.

"Hello?"

"Tim?"

"Alex, where are you? Are you ok?"

Danny started shaking. "Look, I'm in trouble. I hate to get you *involved*, but I don't know what else to do. They've got my mom."

"Who?" Tim asked. "Who's got your mom?"

Danny took a deep breath. "It's a really long story, but here's the short version. The man who killed my dad is trying to kill me, and his team has grabbed my mom. If they don't see me at 5:15, they're going to kill her."

Tim said nothing.

"Tim?" Danny asked. "Are you there?"

"I'm here, don't worry. I'm just trying to understand the whole situation. I knew something was wrong, but I didn't really..."

---

advantage [əd'vɑːntɪdʒ], as a help
to be involved [ɪn'vɒlvd], to be mixed up in something

"I know this is a lot to ask you, but I need help. In about two hours, I have to meet with these people, or they'll kill my mom."

"Dude, they always say that," Tim said. "If you go, they're going to kill you, too." He stopped himself.

Tim just said what Danny already knew. They would kill his mom whether Danny showed up or not. And then they would kill him too.

"I think you've got to call the police," Tim said.

"I can't. They'll kill her."

"Then what are we going to do?"

Danny smiled inside. Tim knew the risks and he still wanted to help. That was real friendship.

"I need some help with the beach area, and I need you to do a few other things. Do you have a piece of paper?"

Tim grabbed some paper and started writing everything down.

As Danny made his way to the beach, everything was planned. He was getting ready to meet up with Steve's men.

Frank and Aaron were sitting outside McDonald's in two different cars. They came to meet Gina here.

"You guys want something to eat?" Gina asked, drinking the last of her Coca Cola.

"No," Aaron said. "I'll wait until afterwards. I want to go over this again."

"Is Eileen still in the trunk?" Frank asked.

"Yes," Gina said with a smile. She was now a blond girl. "Don't worry, I have her right here. She's got enough air to breathe until we need her."

"Good," Frank said.

Aaron was going over the plan again. "Gina, you drive my Mazda around first and check for cops. I'll follow in your car."

5:10. Danny didn't like it. There were fewer cars outside the golf course than he had wished for. Most of the skateboarders and roller bladers had gone home from the beach and it was about to get dark.

The dark would be his friend, he told himself.

From his waiting place next to hole number two on the golf course, Danny watched a green Mazda go down the street for the third time. He knew it would be one of Steve's men, checking out the area for Danny and police. Danny couldn't really see who the driver was.

"Yeah, I'm right here, idiot," Danny whispered through his teeth. He was so nervous, he wanted to throw up.

The Mazda pulled up and stopped across from Danny. A blond female stepped out and left the driver's side of the car with the door open. She spoke with her ice-cold voice: "Hello, Danny."

Danny recognized the voice; it was the woman who had tried to kill him a few hours earlier.

"If it was up to me, I'd shoot you now," Gina said not showing any *emotion.*

Danny couldn't move.

"Look," Gina continued. "Here's the deal." She took her mobile phone out of her pocket. "Your mom will be here in a minute. You'll get to see her and then you need to take a ride and answer some questions."

---

emotion [ɪ'məʊʃn], strong feeling

"Yeah, answer some questions," Danny repeated. "Is that all?"

Gina said, "That depends on how well you answer the questions."

If I get in that car, I'm dead, he thought.

Danny only nodded.

Gina spoke into the phone, and a blue Audi pulled up from a side street and stopped behind the Mazda. A tall, thin man stepped out and walked around to Gina.

Danny recognized Aaron immediately.

Those cold eyes brought back all of his memories from when he was eleven. No way, these guys would get away with this, he suddenly gained new strength.

"Get in," Aaron *commanded.*

"Where's my mother?"

"We'll take you to see her."

"No, I need to see her first, or you'll have to shoot me here," Danny *bluffed.* He knew Aaron wouldn't shoot him there because there were passing cars and still a few skateboarders around. These people are afraid of witnesses, Danny reminded himself. That is why Danny and his mom were being hunted in the first place. And that is what would now keep him alive.

Aaron showed no emotion. Without taking his eyes off Danny, he nodded to Gina, who spoke into the phone.

A gold Honda *entered* the beach area. It stopped about twenty meters behind the Audi. Frank got out and walked around to open the door for Danny's mom. She was now standing next to the car. Her hands were tied and Danny could

---

to command [kəˈmɑːnd], to order
to bluff [blʌf], to pretend something in order to get what you want
to enter, to come into an area

hardly see her face. In a *split second*, it was over. Frank pushed her back into the car and got back into the driver's seat.

"Listen Danny," Aaron said quietly. He opened his jacket with his left hand. He had a gun in his pocket. Then he opened the passenger door. "Get in," he shouted to Danny.

Now a *rider-less* skateboard rolled down the sidewalk toward Aaron.

Danny stepped to the side. "Hey, Aaron," he said back, trying not to sound as scared as he was. "I wonder what's on the skateboard."

---

split second, very quickly
rider-less, without a person on it

Aaron looked at the skateboard. Something small was taped to the top. In black handwriting someone had written "Check out this video."

Aaron removed the small box. It was a mobile phone. He pressed the buttons to play the video. Danny knew that Aaron was watching the recording of himself talking to the driver of the gold Honda. He was also watching how Danny's mother was being thrown into the back of a car.

When Aaron looked up, Danny had a little more control of his voice. "Well, what do you think?"

"I think you should get in the car."

"Really?" Danny said "I thought you would ask what was going on.'"

"No." His eyes were as empty as Danny remembered. "I don't care. You took a video and now I have it. Get in the car." He stepped toward Danny and put his hand on the gun.

"Wow!" Danny shouted. "You're missing *the big picture.*"

Aaron grabbed Danny's arm and pulled him toward the Audi. Gina came closer to help, but Aaron clearly didn't need it.

Danny panicked. This wasn't the way it was supposed to go at all. He had to get through to Aaron somehow. "There are more cameras, Aaron."

Aaron talked while he dragged the boy. "By the time the cops are here, we'll be gone."

"Cops?" Danny looked into Aaron's empty eyes. "Who said anything about cops?"

Suddenly, he had Aaron's attention. "What are you talking about?"

---

the big picture, being aware of what's going on

"I'm talking about the Internet," Danny explained. "I'm talking about putting this on CNN, BBC, YouTube, MySpace, and pretty much anywhere that will let us post this video for the whole world to see."

Aaron gave him a strange look, and then he banged Danny against the car.

"Sure, the police will look for you," Danny said *calmly*. "But I'm sure the terrorists you work for will find you first."

He had Aaron's full attention now.

"I'm also sure that terrorists don't want any publicity. And with the millions of witnesses who will see you throwing a *hostage* into a car, you, Aaron, would have a problem."

---

calm [kɑːm], relaxed
hostage ['hɒstɪdʒ], a kidnapped person

Alex's voice got stronger as he became more *comfortable* with his role. "But do you think your terrorist friends will take any chances? They might think you're a *leak*, so they'll probably have to kill you. I don't think there would be anywhere in the world where you could hide."

Aaron stepped back from the boy. "So what are you offering?"

"The footage, *in exchange for* my mom and me."

Aaron was considering for a few seconds. "How about if I kill you now and then find your little friend with the skateboard and kill him too?"

"Do you think you can find him faster than he can hit 'Send' on his mobile phone?" Danny looked directly into Aaron's eyes. "What do you think? You let two witnesses go, and you avoid two million other witnesses."

Aaron didn't agree. But Danny noticed that he hadn't pulled out his gun either.

"Think about it, Aaron," Danny said "You let us live, we let you live."

"Let's just shoot him now," Gina shouted.

The hate in Aaron's eyes nearly burned a hole in Danny's face.

"Deal," he said to Danny. "Give me the other camera then."

Danny was surprised by Aaron's quick deal. He must have realized that Danny could – and did – have another camera. But he was saving his mom's life and that was what mattered.

"*Untie* my mom and give her a thirty-second walk towards the beach," Danny said. "I'll get the camera for you."

---

comfortable [ˈkʌmfətəbl], at ease or relaxed
leak, here: a spy
in exchange [ɪksˈtʃeɪndʒ] *for*, swapped for
to untie [ʌnˈtaɪ], to release from ropes

Aaron's face was like stone.

"What's the worst thing that could happen? I have no video and you shoot me right here?"

Finally, Aaron dialed Frank on his mobile phone. "Frank, release Eileen. Shut up. I'll explain later. Tell her to walk toward the beach."

Seconds later, Eileen was out of the car and walking across the golf course towards the beach. Danny's eyes followed her until she was out of sight.

After thirty seconds, Aaron said, "Well?"

Danny nodded. With Aaron at his side, he walked back and picked up the camera.

"Here you go."

"Is this it?" Aaron pressed the buttons on the camera and watched part of the video.

"That's it. *Are we good?*"

Aaron nodded. "I'm good." He grabbed Danny's hand, *twisted* it behind his back, and shouted, "Frank, kill the woman."

his hand is twisted behind his back

---

are we good, do we agree

Eileen was confused. She saw Danny talking to Aaron. Nothing *made sense*. She and her son should be dead. Then Frank untied her and told her to walk towards the beach. She ran as fast as she could. She had expected to be shot as soon as she turned her back to him. When there was no shot, she stopped running and turned around to try to see what Danny was doing. Why was he still with Aaron? Was he risking his own life for her? She couldn't let her son do that.

She heard a loud whisper. "Mrs. Miller." Tim was at her side. "Come with me, now!"

"But Danny… "

"He's fine," Tim said. "Come on!"

She ran. Then she heard Aaron's voice: "Kill the woman!" She *sprinted* past the golf course and onto the beach. There, Brian and his four-wheeler were waiting for her.

She turned to Tim, but he was gone.

"Jump on!" Brian shouted and speeded up his car.

Aaron had the camera, the video, the woman, and the boy. He couldn't see the *downside* here. Even if there was another camera around here somewhere, he would hide the truth by changing the video. Misinformation he would call it in court.

"Gina, we're out of here," he ordered, as he pushed Danny

---

to make sense, to be logical
to sprint, to run fast
downside, negative result

onto the car again. This whole *operation* had taken nearly seven minutes. He couldn't risk this taking any more time.

His phone rang.

"Aaron, she got away!" Frank shouted in his ear.

"What?"

Aaron didn't hear the rest. Something hit his car. *Bullets.* No. *Marbles* maybe? When the frozen paintballs hit, Danny took the chance to sprint away from Aaron. He had hardly taken two steps when Aaron grabbed him. He smashed Danny's head backward. "I never liked you, Danny," he shouted into Danny's face.

Danny's right hand had already found his weapon. He buried his pen into Aaron's upper *thigh.* He missed the *artery* he was aiming for, but he heard a cry from Aaron.

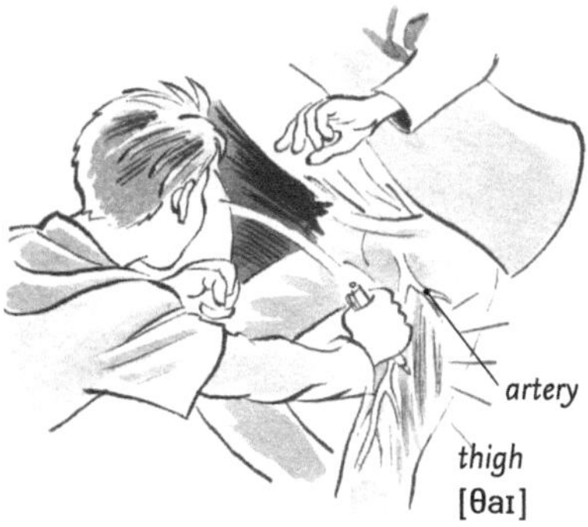

Aaron felt the *massive* pain moving from his leg and up his spine, into his face. He pulled the trigger. He wanted to shoot that boy right now.

Aaron only saw a glimpse of the skateboard before it smashed into his nose. His head hit the cement, then he blacked out.

"Aaron!" a woman's voice screamed.

Danny saw Gina sprinting toward him from across the street.

---

operation [ɒpəˈreɪʃn], planned event
marble [ˈmɑːbəl], small glass ball used in games
massive [ˈmæsɪv], very strong or big

He thought that would give him enough time to run onto the golf course and a better chance to hide.

He heard Gina make her pistol ready.

Then, he heard the sweetest sound in the world.

Sirens! – Many police cars were now on both ends of the street.

Danny didn't watch them all being arrested. He only saw Gina being *handcuffed*, that was all he needed to see.

He picked up the camera from the sidewalk and walked toward Tim's hiding place next to the golf course.

"Thanks for calling the cops, Tim!"

His friend came out and smiled. "Sometimes you just need to call for backup." He handed Danny his mobile phone. "It's for you."

Danny grabbed it. "Hi, mom. Yeah, I'm ok."

Danny could hardly move. He was too tired to do anything. When he heard the sound of Brian's engine again, he smiled. His friends had *stood by him*, and his mom was safe.

It was time they had a talk.

---

to be handcuffed [ˈhændkʌft], to be put in police chains
to stand by, to help or to back up

Chapter 26

Steve Ballantine was still waiting in the Illinois prison for his appeal date to come up.

He couldn't believe how badly his team had handled this job. It was planned perfectly. Get one little kid – what was so hard about that? Idiots. Aaron and Gina were in jail. They *deserved* what they got. That was the *price of failure.*

Luckily, both Frank and Leah had been smart enough to escape. As soon as it was safe, they would contact him, and then they would find Danny again. Steve knew that there would be no chance that the board would release him after this. But then there was the next appeal date to plan for.

Marcus sat down next to Steve. His friends followed.

"Is there something I can do for you?" Steve said with his tough smile. Marcus knew the rules. If he wanted Steve to arrange to get hold of information or *supplies,* he had to be *discreet.* Usually he just gave Steve a shopping list. He never brought friends.

"Yes, there is," Marcus said as he smiled to a guard. "I saw an interesting video."

Steve *stiffened.* "Hey, that mess didn't involve me."

"But it involved your men," Marcus continued. "We are all only as strong as our *weakest link.*"

---

to deserve [dɪ'zɜːv], to earn or have the right to something
price of failure ['feɪljə], the cost of losing
supply [sə'plaɪ], item or commodity
to be discreet [dɪ'skriːt], to be careful about what you say
to stiffen, here: to be unable to move for a short time
weakest link, the most useless person

Steve blushed.

Now Marcus lifted his wrist to show Steve a sharp knife hidden in his sleeve. Steve sat quietly he knew he was being warned! It would only be a matter of time before somebody used that knife to kill him.

Frank felt free for the first time in weeks. Like Leah beside him, he had changed his hair color. Their colored contact lenses and *tanned bodies* completed their *disguises.* He and Leah would stay in *Saba* for the week to look for a place to buy with the money his crew had earned. He didn't think the rest of the team would need the money while they were locked up in jail. He and Leah would never go back to the United States, though. They would live here forever with enough money to relax and put the past behind them.

They would start a new life.

From binoculars many cars away, their killer watched Frank and Leah get out of their car. He then followed them into their hotel - all ready to shoot.

Danny and Eileen were back in their house. "Mom, I'm going to Tim's. We're going to skate until dark."

---

tanned bodies, bodies turned brown by the sun
disguise [dɪz'gaɪz], object used to change your appearance like a wig and sunglasses
Saba, tourist island in the Netherlands Antilles

"Ok. But remember, Danny, dinner is around six o'clock!" Eileen shouted from the kitchen window.

The last few weeks had been tough. The police had interviewed them at least ten times. *Lawyers* asked them all sorts of questions. Danny and his friends had uploaded the video to every site that would let them. With a simple video-editing program, Danny was able to change the faces of anyone in the video he didn't want the world to recognize. It was time for Danny and his mom to be themselves and create real lives, not new identities. They needed time to sit back and realize that the Torberts were the Torberts again. Danny and Eileen needed to find out exactly what that meant. For now, it was time to stop running. It was time to do a lot of biking, four-wheeling, and skateboarding.

It was time for playing a fair game.

Danny opened the door and jumped on his skateboard, ready for his own real life.

---

lawyer ['lɔɪə], legal representative

Questions

Chapter 1

Think about Alex and Sonya Miller:

- What do you think Alex and Sonya are doing? A) Could they be on the run from the police? Or B) could they be hiding from somebody?
- What new identity does Alex decide to have?
- What new colour of hair does Sonya change to?
- How many social security numbers does Sonya say she has left?

Chapter 2 and Chapter 3

Think about the situation when Frank is visiting Steve in jail:

- What are Frank and Steve talking about?
- Use a digital camera or your camera on your mobile phone. Make a photo or a drawing to show what you think the front page picture of the New York newspaper looks like. Make sure you show how you think Danny looks and what he does on the picture.
- Alex's mum has the latest computer equipment. What does she use the computer for and who supplied it?
- Describe Sonya and Alex's new car.
- Why did they buy a new car?
- How did they buy it.
- What brand is their new car?

Think about when Frank comes back to visit Steve in jail:

- What does Steve want Frank to get him and why?
- What does Steve want Frank to do on Google Earth?
- What does he hope to find?

Click into Google earth yourself:

- See if you can find Virginia Beach. Are you able to see any people or cars?

Describe how Alex and Tim are getting along:

- Make a mini dialogue between Alex and Tim, where they talk about their new after school project in Tim's backyard. Make sure you use the words "dude" and "cool" in your dialogue.

Who is Brian?

- How does Brian act towards Alex and why?
- Draw a sketch of the situation in the hallway where Alex first meets Brian.
- Describe your sketch to a partner. Discuss how you think Alex's and Brain's relation will develop from there.

Chapter 7

Think about Tom Lankford:

- Make a brainstorm.
- Write down as many descriptive words as you can think of to describe Tom Lankford.
- Write a characteristic of Tom Lankford where you use as many of your descriptive words as possible.

Make sure you mention:

- Who Tom Lankford works for?
- What his job is now?
- What his job was before?

Chapter 8 and Chapter 9

Imagine the situation where Alex and his new friends are building a new ramp:

- Alex and his friends use a lot of "skateboarder slang." Find the skateboard slang words in the text.
- See if there are any skateboarders in your class who can explain what each term means. If not, study the explanations and drawings in the book.

Think about the boys' trip to Mount Trashmore:

- How do they get there?
- Why is the skateboard park called Mount Trashmore?
- What is Alex afraid to do when he gets there?

Chapter 10 and Chapter 11

- Brian gets accused of letting off firecrackers but who did Alex see do it?
- Discus Alex' "dilemma" with a partner!
- Should he tell the headteacher who actually did it?
- How do you imagine the other kids will react if he does?
- Alex gets Brian out of trouble. How does Brian react?

Play the dialogue between Brian and Alex as it's described in the book. Then add your own twist to the dialogue like:
A) Alex doesn't want to accept Brian's thank you
B) Brian is to tough to say thank you
C) How would you ideally like the situation to turn out?

- What does Brian invite Alex to do sometime?

Think about the situation in Tom Lankford's car:
- What is the name of the gunman who hides in Tom Lankford's car?
- What does he want?
- Why does Lankford not save himself?
- Look in the text and write down the considerations that go through Lankford's mind.
- Discuss the morals of his decision in groups.

Chapter 12, Chapter 13, chapter 14, chapter 15, chapter 16

Imagine the situation where Rick Torbert is shot dead.
- What happened to Alex's father?
- What happened to Alex?
- Try and write a diary note as if it was Alex's diary description of the day his dad was killed. How did the day start, what happened during the day and how did the day end? Follow the situation in the text and add your personal comments and thoughts.
- What is Ed doing to find Alex's address?
- Why does Alex's mom buy two new mobile phones and why does she pay cash when she buys them?
- What is Gina's job?

- Look at a map of the USA and point out where Gina and her team have been searching for Danny and Eileen. Point out where Virginia Beach is on the map as well.

Your opinion on crime?:
- What is Brian's dad wearing around his leg?
- Why is he wearing it?
- Is that a good solution?
- What does Rick think about terrorism?

Discuss with a partner what you think of the following crimes. Are some more serious than others?:
Put them in order 1 to 6 with number 1 for the most serious crime.
How would you punish each person? Explain why.
- A terrorist whose bomb kills five people and hurts forty.
- A bank robber who shoots dead an armed policeman.
- A drunk driver who kills a child in a road accident.
- A wife who buys a gun and kills her violent husband.
- A gunman who goes crazy and shoots ten people in a shop.
- A crazy gunman who shoots ten children in a school.

Compare the crimes on the list to what crimes are committed in the story so fare.

Chapter 17

- How many single parents does Ed find in November?
- Gina has found Alex. How did she do it?

Chapter 18

Imagine the situation where Alex meets Gina at his new school.

- Why is Alex so nervous about the interview with Gina?
- What is the interview about?
- What colour is the Buick Gina drives?
- Look up the model online. Do you think it's a nice car? In your own words give a description of the car.

Chapter 19 and Chapter 20

Think about the situation when Alex gets away from the school.

- How does he get away?
- Is Gina still around?
- When Gina crashed into the lamppost and wrecked her car, can you tell what the lamppost was made of?
- Gina pretends she is injured, a nice man offers to bring her to hospital.
- Can you remember what type of car he drives?

Chapter 21

- Alex tells his mom they have been found. Where do they agree to meet?
- Make a role play where you act out what happens when Alex's mom gets home.

Chapter 22

- What text message does Gina type into her phone?
- Alex's mom does not turn up. How does he know she is not coming?
- Where is Sonya (Eileen) being hidden?
- Danny wants to meet Gina and her men on the boardwalk but they end up somewhere else. Why is that? Do you know where they agree to meet?
- What time do they agree to meet?

Chapter 23

Think about how Tim and Danny make a plan to save Danny's mom.

- Why does Danny not call the Police?
- Break into groups. Come up with a plan to save Eileen.
- Gina has changed her hair colour! What does she look like now?

Chapter 24

- What does Danny see go down the street three times?
- Why will Danny not get in Aaron's car?
- What is Danny waiting for?
- Aaron opens his jacket! What's inside?
- What is on the skateboard?
- Danny and Aaron make a deal. Can you describe it?
- Tell what happens next.

Chapter 25

- Eileen ran towards the sea. What was she expecting to happen?
- Who was waiting for her?
- Aaron is thinking he won the battle. Explain why.
- Something starts hitting the car and breaking the glass. What do you think it is?
- How does Danny get away from Aaron?
- What does Danny hit Aaron with?
- Danny hears a sound he likes, what is it?

Chapter 26

- What happens to Steve?
- What happens to Frank and Leah?
- Now the killers have been caught what do you think Danny and his mom will do?

The title of the book is 'Fakie': this is to mean somebody who is pretending to be someone they are not.

Using the word PRETEND.

- Make as many words as you can from the seven letters. E.G. END!

Imagine you are Danny and Eileen.

- Where do you think they will go in life?
- In your own words tell their future story.

- The letters below form words used in the book. What words are they?

  ylqiute
  tbakeadrser
  urdg
  tcucsa
  vecide
  tiryescu
  lscooh
  llintapsb
  smrooacls
  lagilor

TEEN READERS NOW AVAILABLE:

Ann Halam: The Shadow on the Stairs (0)
Philip Hewitt: Emma and the Boy Next Door (0)
Alan Posener: The Double Life of a Very Black Cat (1)
Jeremy Taylor: All 4 Love (1)
Jeremy Taylor: Dr. Schnitzler's Dog (1)
Pete Johnson: Runaway Teacher (1)
Stephen Speight: Bed and Breakfast (1)
Stephen Speight: The Runaway (1)
Wolf and Ferro: The Missing Mascot (1)
Annie Dalton: Friday Forever (2)
E.E. Richardson: Black Bones (2)
George Ivanoff: The Bookworm Mystery (2)
James Heneghan: Hit Squad (2)
James Heneghan & Norma Charles: Bank Job (2)
Jeremy Taylor: Football Friends (2)
Jeremy Taylor: Luke (2)
Karen McCombie: Love is the Drug (2)
Kevin Brooks: Johnny Delgado (2)
Lee Weatherly: Them (2)
Paul Davenport: Horror Trip on the Pecos River (2)
Philip Hewitt: Helping Hands (2)
Philip Hewitt: Terror in the Hills (2)
Stephen Speight: Summer School Adventures (2)
Stephen Speight: The Fjord Murder (2)
Tony Varrato: Fakie (2)
Alan Posener: Oh Carol and Other Steve Stories (3)
Anne Cassidy: Talking to Strangers (3)
Charles Ferro: Horror at Remsen High (3)
Charles Ferro: Kool 1 (3)
Charles Ferro: Moonstruck (3)
Charles Ferro: Voodoo Zombies (3)
Chris Carter: Grizzly Attack (3)
Jeremy Taylor: Love me Blindly (3)
Paul Davenport: Crossroads to Love (3)
Paul Davenport: Snakeman (3)
Philip Hewitt: Quest for a Father (3)
Sylvia Olsen: Yellow Line (3)
Charles Ferro: Forever Young (4)
Charles Ferro: Over the Line (4)
Holly-Jane Rahlens: One Fine Day (4)
Philip Hewitt: Secrets (4)

Find all titles at **easyreaders.eu**.